THE PRACTICAL GUIDE TO LITERATURE

by

David Cockburn
English Department
High School of Dundee

ISBN 0 7169 6021 4

ROBERT GIBSON · Publisher
17 Fitzroy Place, Glasgow, G3 7SF, Scotland, U.K.

CONTENTS

INTRODUCTION

Although this book is written to help you with Higher English – the Literature Unit and the Examination itself – nevertheless it is geared really to any course concerning literary studies. It is geared at the Higher Level, though it will be of help to those candidates also studying Intermediate Level. The book gives you advice about and techniques for the study of literature and the last two chapters give you sound, practical advice about your Specialist Study, the Critical Essay, and the examination itself.

The most important aspect of any English course is literature – it is the very foundation upon which courses are built. The problem often is that many young people feel alienated by literature, convinced that "great works" are not for them. Even the term "a work of literary merit" is enough to put them off. Writers such as Shakespeare or Tennyson or Charlotte Brontë or Charles Dickens or Philip Larkin seem detached from our society and remote from the experience of many people, especially the young, at the beginning of the twenty-first century.

It is a point worth considering, however, that authors write about human nature; their concerns are our concerns, the situations they create and characters they invent are very similar to the situations and characters with which we are familiar. I have always argued that much of human wisdom is expressed in imaginative literature – and Oscar Wilde once commented that life is a cheap imitation of art!

We are all concerned about the problems that face us just because we have been born – problems of personal identity, problems that face the young, problems that arise from our relationships with other people.

Literature isn't dead or remote or isolated. Books aren't museum pieces. Literature needs to be read as if it were alive, as if it were speaking directly to us, the reader. After all, *Hamlet* is as popular today as it must have been in Shakespeare's time, nearly four hundred years ago. The play has survived simply because it has something enduring to say about the human condition and human experience that is as relevant today as it was to an Elizabethan audience.

I do recognise, however, that it takes time and effort and skill to read works of "literary merit". I cannot give you the time nor can I get round the need for effort: but I can offer you the skills that you require. That is the purpose of this book. I trust that it will help bring literature alive for you, help you to see its relevance in our fast and changing society, and above all help you to recognise its tremendous ability to help you reflect on and understand the human condition.

CHAPTER ONE

THE ROLE OF TEXTUAL ANALYSIS

Why do we read fiction — novels, short stories? One of the answers must be: "for pleasure". But there are other reasons, one of the most important of which is that, from the ideas that a book of fiction contains, we can learn something about ourselves, about others, and about the society in which the book is set. In other words, we learn about life.

There are two main reasons why we read (or watch plays or view films): to confirm our experience and to extend our experience. Often we enjoy a book because we identify with one of the main characters in it — he / she has the same background as ourselves or is going through the same experiences or is confronted with the same problems. In the middle of such a book we can find ourselves quite surprised by one of the character's reactions to a situation that we ourselves have recently experienced — to such an extent that we declare to ourselves: "But that's exactly how I felt last Tuesday . . .". The book, then, is confirming our experience, making us a bit more aware of how we feel, how we behave, how we are as people. Since all of us (quite naturally) are interested in self, we enjoy these books because they are saying something about self, even although what is said is coming through the made-up experiences of a character who exists only in the imagination.

I said that there were two reasons for reading. The other reason is that we enjoy having our experience extended: the novel, perhaps, occupies a world which we don't know, but which we are keen to learn about or it involves a character who is experiencing situations / problems / emotions which we have not undergone, but by which we are fascinated. We may not know what it's like to be a brutish, over-bearing general who murders his king and then rules tyrannically, yet we may read *Macbeth* to find out; in fact, we may well enjoy *Macbeth* precisely because we are not like that.

More than likely the two reasons come together in the same book, but nevertheless our enjoyment of a book can be ascribed to one or other or both of these reasons. Clearly, then, the books we read and enjoy (or don't read because we're bored by them) say quite a lot about ourselves. If we read a book because it confirms our experience, then that says something about the experiences we have undergone; it also says something about us that we enjoy reliving the experiences or reflecting on the experiences of others through the book we are reading.

Literature, then, poses a problem for young people: if the enjoyment of reading depends on the experiences of the reader, then how can young people, who just because they are young and therefore haven't accumulated much in the way of adult experience, how can these young people enjoy books? Much of what is presented in the way of literature to 17-year-olds really does require adult experience before it can be fully appreciated. This is not to patronise the young or to be superior to them — it is merely a fact of life. How can a 17-year-old identify with a 60-year-old salesman who is tired to the death? How can a 40-year-old for that matter understand what it's like to be an 80-year-old king who has given away his kingdom to ungrateful daughters? Yet clearly young people appreciate *Death of a Salesman* and the early middle-aged enjoy *King Lear*. So we need to bring more than just experience to literature: we need the ability to imagine the experiences of others and to understand how they think and feel. In so doing, we extend our imagination and develop our understanding. Literature, then, can help us grow and mature as human beings. Wisdom isn't just a quality to be found in literature: literature can be a means of developing wisdom in the reader.

I have spent some time stressing the importance and function of reading — if it can be said to have a function, that is. You must not think of *Hamlet* or *To Kill a Mockingbird* or *Afternoons* as Fifth Year texts suitable for Higher English, to be swallowed whole and regurgitated in the examination, but as experiences valuable in themselves and valuable in the contribution they can make to your development as a human being. What matters is your relationship with the texts you intend to study in your Higher English course — what they mean to you as an individual, what you get out of them. That means, of course, that you must be very familiar with the texts and that you have to spend a lot of time working out what they do mean to you. Once you have done that, then you can begin on the process of asking yourself how — the means by which — the author has brought about in you the reactions that he has. The entire process is circular, however — as you get to know the text, the more you realise what it means to you, and the more you know what it means to you, the more you are aware of the techniques by which the author has brought about the reaction he / she has in you, and the more you are aware of the author's technique, the more you get to know the text. And so on and so on . . .

Getting to know texts in this way obviously cannot be done the night before the examination — it has to be done as you study the text in class, using your time at home to read, reread, reflect and respond.

When it comes to studying any work of literature, film, television play, soap opera, whatever, bear in mind three questions which correspond to the stages previously outlined:

> *(a)* What is the novel / play / poem / film about?
> *(Getting to know the text.)*
>
> *(b)* What effects does it have on me?
> *(How do I react — cry, laugh, feel sad, feel bored?)*
>
> *(c)* How are the effects achieved?
> *(What techniques has the author used to bring about this reaction in me?)*

It has to be stressed, and it will be throughout this book, that skills in English aren't discrete — separate and compartmentalised. As we develop one skill, we affect the development of another. I've already referred to the circularity of the reading process outlined above. It is the same with three questions: our ability to answer *(a)* makes the answering of *(b)* easier, and our skills at working out *(c)* will, in turn, help us redefine our answer to *(a)*, and so on. But *(c)*, the more perceptive of you will have already worked out, is really Textual Analysis!

In other words, by studying literature as suggested above you are sharpening your skills of Textual Analysis, and as you do that, you develop your reading skills and make the study of literature more rewarding. And the more we develop reading skills the more our writing skills are affected — but that is another story!

I want to say a bit more about these three questions and how they will help you with the reading process. The questions, when you think about it, are fairly obviously based on the way we react to any piece of literature or film. They are really questions that are aimed at making our subconscious reactions to literature as explicit as possible. When you watch a film or read a book, it is only natural to say to yourself — or to your friends — what you think it is about, and, of course, you have a reaction which you may not state but which you will *feel*. You will have laughed or cried or felt sad or made to think things that you had never thought before. In other words, you will have provided *implicitly* the answer to questions *(a)* and *(b)*.

But let's take things a stage further. Let's tease out these questions until we make them highly explicit and your answers to them highly articulate. The answer to question *(a)* is not an answer based on a retelling of the plot but is an answer based on the ideas or concerns or issues or *themes* of the text. Now you will be delighted to hear that literature really only ever deals with three themes — birth, marriage, and death.

CHAPTER TWO

THEMES IN LITERATURE

Let me explain each of these themes in a bit more detail. Most of the fiction or poetry that we read or the drama that we see in the theatre or the soaps and films that we watch on television all deal with the problems that occur just because we are human. Just think for a minute about the latest episode of *Eastenders* or *Coronation Street* and you will see what I mean: both soaps will be dealing with some problem (or issue or concern or theme) that stems from the human condition. These problems fall into the three broad areas — birth, marriage, and death.

Let's take each in turn. By *birth* I mean, of course, the act of being born and you can think of a number of stories that involve the birth of a child. But by *birth* I also mean the problems that stem from our being born — the problems that we come across just because we are here on the planet. Many of these problems you will already have experienced: questions such as *Why am I here? What makes me the person I am? What will become of me? What is life about?* And all the other problems that, particularly, adolescence brings. Because you are young, all things are possible — your ambitions can be limitless. Literature and film often deal with the problems that occur just because we are on the planet and are young.

By *marriage*, I mean more than just the conventional relationship between men and women. I include under the general title *marriage* all relationships — relationships with the opposite sex, relationships with friends, relationships with parents, with older people, with younger people, with authority figures. How many problems stem from relationships? Think of all the major concerns we have — love, hate, betrayal, jealousy, envy, unrequited love, power, corruption — all stem from our relationships with other people.

And, finally, by *death I mean* more than just the act of dying, though think of the number of novels, short stories, films that deal with the very act of someone dying and the consequences for the living. But I include under the title *death* old age — something most of you won't have to worry about for a very long time. The trouble is that old age comes more quickly than you think and brings with it a time for reflection! Just as young people reflect on what will become of them, so the middle and older aged reflect on what has become of them, what have they done with their life, could it have been better, and how best can they spend the time that remains to them? What also strikes older people is the looming certainty of death and all that it implies — what happens to me when I am dead, is there life after death or is it a bit like pulling the plug from a television set, leaving nothing but emptiness? Think of the recent number of films that have dealt with ghosts and the supernatural and their relationship with the living!

These then are the themes with which literature deals. But what is vitally important to remember is that it is your opinion that matters — whatever theme you detect is the theme that matters. And you have to build up the confidence to be able to state what theme you think the novel, poem, play or film is dealing with, remembering that all you have to be able to do is justify that theme by referring to the text. Don't rely on someone else telling you what the theme is — stand up for yourself and say what you think it is.

But I said earlier that we had to think about all three questions — and the second question is *What effects does it have on me?* I think this is just as important a question as the other two — after all, if we are really interested in what we are reading or watching we will continue to read and watch, driven not only to find out what happens next — though that is important — but also because the material has captured our imagination and our emotions. So our reaction matters — whether we laugh or cry or feel saddened or frightened or tense or disappointed or even bored. Remember I said that we often read — or watch films — to confirm our experience? I think that needs to be explained a bit more. Experience, when you think about it, is by its nature entirely private. Everything that we experience comes via our senses — sight, sound, touch, smell, and taste — and since those senses are unique to every one of us, it follows that no-one else can share in the experiences that these senses are providing. In fact, the only way that we can "share" experience is by talking about it: that is we have to use words. Now I also think that since life is fast, unpredictable, and random (or seemingly random), then our experience is also chaotic: often we don't have time or the inclination to examine, analyse, or reflect on our experiences. But an author can and does reflect on his or her heightened awareness of experience.

What has all this to do with literature, you may ask. Well, let's begin with how an author comes to write a book. Obviously, it is impossible to plumb the depths of any author's psyche to find out what demon has driven him to fill a page with writing, but something can be said about the process. All authors really do write from experience, but unlike the rest of us they are really very acutely aware of their own experience. They reflect on it, analyse it, dissect it. They also have a heightened sensitivity, together, obviously, with developed articulacy — i.e., they can use words. Words become the symbols the author uses to recreate those experiences so that the novel, the play, the poem then becomes the symbolic representation of his experiences. Put another way, the writer is encoding his experience in words and symbols created by the words.

When we, on the other, read the text we reverse the process — we decode the words and symbols using our own experience. In a work of art, then, the author isn't communicating directly with the reader: he depends on the reader's own experiences and, to a large extent, he repatterns, reorganises the reader's experiences. Now if the reader has limited experience, or is unaware of his experiences, then that reader will become easily bored with what the author has written because the author will be making demands of the reader which the reader is unable to meet. Similarly, of course, the reader can make demands of a text which the author is unable to meet — the text can be too simplistic and dull!

So when I say that we should be aware of the effects a text has on us, I am saying that we should be aware of our experience being reworked, repatterned, reorganised by the text. All we can bring to a text is our experience, and our understanding of that text will be in terms of that experience. Obviously intelligence, imagination and our own facility with words all play a part, but in the main, our concern is with experience. Our experience will inevitably change and develop as we mature, and, accordingly, our relationship with the text will change, develop, and mature. What we feel when we read *The Whitsun Weddings* at 18 years of age won't be what we feel when we read the same poem at 58 years of age.

Let me finish with a little story that should illustrate what I have been talking about. When I was at school (many decades ago), my Higher English course was made up of pretty tedious stuff, taught very badly. Throughout the year, every Tuesday for two periods we studied *Hamlet*. "Studied" is not quite the right word: it was a line by line plough through with the teacher dictating notes about what each line, scene and Act meant. I was bored beyond belief. The text meant nothing and all I had to show for it were reams of notes that meant even less. Then one dull, wet Saturday in the middle of a Lanarkshire winter, I decided to read *Hamlet* for myself, this time on my own terms. Suddenly, the play became alive and three-dimensional for me: I realised that it wasn't about revenge or procrastination. It was for me about an intelligent, sensitive, articulate young man who was surrounded by "thickies". I knew exactly how Hamlet felt! That Saturday afternoon taught me something about the nature of literature that no English teacher had ever managed to teach me. Literature could be alive and personal and about how I feel — in other words, it was alive and all about experience and was not about a set of dictated notes. That discovery has never left me.

I hope that anecdote helps you see what I am getting at. Use your experience when you read, and don't be afraid of your reactions as long as they are your honest reactions.

The intellectually demanding question is: how have these reactions been brought about? We've now come to question *(c)*, which is the business of Textual Analysis. *How were these effects achieved?* How has the author put the text together? What techniques has the author used to create the effects he has achieved?

Literature is art, and, as with all art, it is artificially constructed — it is designed and put together by someone in a particular and definite way. Therefore, it is quite possible, with a great deal of skill, to examine how it has been put together; that is the function of Textual Analysis and the job of students of all literary forms. That may seem to you almost a cold-hearted and destructive thing to do, like a scientist dispassionately dissecting tissue. But it is not really like that: literature, especially poetry, often deals with very complex emotions, attitudes and experiences in a way so compressed as to render it immediately inaccessible to a reader — it is unlikely that you will discover all that there is to discover in a poem at the first or even the tenth reading. You need to make an effort to gain a fuller understanding, and the analysis of the techniques the author has used, far from destroying his art, should enhance it and allow the work to make its fullest impact on you.

In order, then, to study literature what sorts of techniques do we need to know about? Obviously they differ according to the text itself: a novel will demand a knowledge of setting and characterisation; a play of plot, interpretation of character, and analysis of dramatic conflict; a poem of verse structure and rhythm — though, of course, there is overlap. But you need above all to have a knowledge of language and the way it works. And that is where we will begin next.

CHAPTER THREE

LINGUISTIC AND LITERARY TECHNIQUES

In order to read effectively, we need to be able to do more than merely decode the letters. We need to have an understanding of language and the way it works. Let's begin with grammar, which is the term we give to the way in which words form a recognisable pattern. For example, you instantly recognise the following arrangement of words:

I went into the cafe and bought a Coke.

You would still recognise the following rearrangement:

Into the cafe I went and bought a Coke

or even:

Into the cafe I went and a Coke I bought

but you would have difficulty with:

A into Coke the Cafe I went bought I and

Your difficulty is because the above sentence has broken all the rules of grammar.

There are, then, rules of grammar which govern the ways in which we arrange words to make that arrangement meaningful. The rules are to do with the connections between words and the function of each word in the sentence.

First of all, let's look at the table below to see how we label words:

Parts of Speech

Part of Speech	Explanation	Example
Concrete noun	The name of something which actually exists and can be seen, heard, touched, etcetera.	Lion, human, pen, star, chair, moon, sun, nose, ear
Abstract noun	The name of an emotion or feeling —something that you cannot touch,	Happiness, sadness, tiredness, grief, excitement, hearing, eyesight, loveliness, beauty, nosiness, cleanliness, uprightness, merriment, backwardness, intelligence, boredom, freedom, martyrdom, kingdom, earldom
Proper Noun	A person's name — the name of a town, country, city	Aberdeen, Scotland, Kevin, Fiona
Collective noun	The name given to a group of animals or objects	A pack. of wolves, a. flock of sheep, a herd of cows. a bunch of flowers, a pride of lions, a gaggle of geese
Adjective	A word which describes things or people	Beautiful, pretty, excited, tired, happy, sad, clever, intelligent, bored
Compound Adjective	A word made up of two words (hyphenated) to describe something or person	Long-blind, hunchback-born, half-paralysed

Part of Speech	Explanation	Example
Adverb	A word which modifies or alters the meaning of the verb — in English the adverb almost always ends in -ly, but watch out for words such as "then", "however", "moreover" — which are also adverbs	Beautifully, lovely, playfully, excitedly, merrily, happily, sadly, tiredly, slowly, bluntly
Verb	Difficult to define, though the best definition is the *doing word*. Sometimes verbs do not *do*, however, such as the verb *to be*.	To skip, to run, to jump, to think, to speak, to write, to spell, to understand, to read, to play, to look, to cross, to hear, to touch, to swim
Present participle	The -ing word when it is part of the verb	I am running, walking, jumping
Conjunctions	Linking or joining words	And, because, but, or, since
Prepositions	Words which indicate relationships between objects	On, under, below, on top, beside, beneath, above, through, into, at, in
Prepositional Phrase	A phrase which begins with a preposition — often at the beginning of a sentence	In the morning, on the sink, on the table, at the pictures, in the classroom, in France, on the sea, under the bed, beside the coffee table, above the mantelpiece, below the chair, with the books

Part of Speech	Explanation	Example
Definite article	The word "the"	The lion, the boy, the car, the bus, the new livery
Indefinite article	The words "a" and "an".	An apple, a flock of sheep, a gaggle of schoolboys, a collection of books
Gerund	Where the word ending -ing acts as a noun	A pedestrian crossing, a walking stick
Pronoun	The words which stand for nouns	He, she, we, you, they, them, his, hers, theirs, our, ours, yours, mine, it, its, your
Comparative adjectives	Where you have the adjective, the comparative and the superlative	Good, better, best, bad, worse, worst, happy, happier, happiest

It is useful to know about the parts of speech since it is much easier to talk about, say, a present participle than it is to try and describe what the function of the word ending in -ing is in the overall sentence!

The rules of grammar allow only a certain order of words — you can say, for example, *into the* but not *the into*. The point of all this is, firstly, that you should know about nouns, adjectives, verbs and so on, and, secondly, that you should also know that when words are in a grammatical arrangement then there is a meaningful context — that is, the terms are laid down by which we can work out the meaning of any given word. For example:

I reached the bar where I was to have a drink with my friend.

We know the meaning of the word "bar" by examining the context; the word "drink" suggests that the "bar" isn't a wall bar in a gym. Further, we know that the "drink" in this example probably isn't a Coke. The context reveals all!

All of us can operate these rules without being aware of them, but for the purpose of the study of literature — and Textual Analysis in particular — we need to become aware of the rules and how they operate. The meaning of a word in a sentence, then, is determined by its relationship with the other words in that sentence.

The other thing you need to know is that words have two levels of meaning — denotation and connotation. The denotation of a word is the actual "thing" or object to which the word refers. When I say "There's my dog chasing your cat", then the denotation of "dog" is my actual dog and the denotation of "cat" is your cat which my dog is chasing. The connotation of a word, on the other hand, is the picture conjured up in our mind, by our associations with a particular word and our experiences of it.

Look carefully at the following list of words and. in the space provided jot down whatever comes into your head. Don't spend too much time thinking about it.

Bottle	
Apple	
Fire	
School	
Sea	
Girl	
Book	
Food	

Now against "Bottle" you might have written "milk", "glass", "green", "beer" or even "ship". None of these responses is wrong — each response is determined by our experience of the word and what you associate with it. Look carefully at all ten of *your* words — these are for you the connotations of each of the ten words above. Again, although all ten words are in our language, and are, therefore, shared by all of us, each connotation is unique and private because each connotation depends on our experiences of and associations with the word.

Much of language operates at the level of connotation, particularly the language of poetry. When we read a poem we should allow our imaginations to work on the words and images so that we are aware of the connotations. For example,

His secret murders sticking on his hands. (from 'Macbeth')

Think of what "sticking" suggests to you, and think of what the idea of a murder "sticking" to someone's hands suggests.

But also remember what I said about the rules of language and how the meaning of one word is affected / determined by the meaning of other words in the same sentence. Although poetry operates at the level of connotation, nevertheless the area of connotation of a word is limited, or circumscribed, by the context of the sentence or the image. We know that in the sentence:

I went into the bar and bought a drink

the connotations of the word "bar" (which might have included chocolate, metal, gold, prison) are nevertheless restricted by the context. By the same token, sometimes we have to go to the context in order to understand the connotations of an image. Look at the following example and you will see what I mean:

The star-eaten blanket of the sky.

That image may appear difficult, even meaningless, or, indeed, it may cause our imaginations to run riot, producing in us a kind of startled awareness because of its freshness. But given that the context of the image is a poem about a tramp sleeping on the Embankment and given the association of "star-eaten" with "moth-eaten" then the meaning of the line becomes clearer.

In other words, although I say you cannot be wrong when you respond to "bottle" with the word "milk", nevertheless you cannot make just any response to a word or image in a poem: you have to take account of the connotative meaning of such a word as defined by the overall context.

Meaning, then, has to do with the structure of a sentence and the connotative areas of words within that sentence, though the two are obviously incredibly closely linked and the one affects the other. The structure of a sentence, however, can considerably affect meaning. For example, contrast

> *I walked into the classroom and I saw the overturned desks, the broken chairs, the waste paper on the floor and the writing on the wall.*

with

> *I walked into the classroom and I saw the overturned desks and the broken chairs and the waste paper on the floor and the writing on the wall.*

The difference between the two sentences is one of structure: the first is a list in conventional form with the "and" (we can now use the term *conjunction*) between the penultimate and last items, whereas the second sentence uses the conjunction between each item. But what difference does that make? The first list is in haphazard order — you can interchange the items without really affecting meaning. But in the second list, the conjunction suggests that each item is linked to the one which has gone before in a significant way: "writing on the wall" takes on almost a metaphorical meaning, as though some disaster is implied by the gradual build-up of items in the list. In other words, the structure with the conjunctions (polysyndetic structure) suggests or connotes something sinister in a way in which the structure without the conjunctions (asyndetic structure) does not.

Let's put what we have learned into practice. Read carefully the following extract from the opening of *Under Milk Wood*, a play by Dylan Thomas. We will concentrate on connotation and structure:

UNDER MILK WOOD

[Silence]

FIRST VOICE (Very softly}

To begin at the beginning:

It is spring, moonless night in the small town, starless and bible-black, the cobblestreets silent and the hunched, courters'-and-rabbits' wood limping invisible down to the sloeblack, slow, black, crowblack, fishingboat-bobbing sea. The houses are blind as moles (though moles see fine to-night in the snouting, velvet dingles) or blind as Captain Cat there in the muffled middle by the pump and the town clock, the shops in mourning, the Welfare Hall in widows' weeds. And all the people of the lulled and dumbfound town are sleeping now.

Hush, the babies are sleeping, the farmers, the fishers, the tradesmen and pensioners, cobbler, school-teacher, postman and publican, the undertaker and the fancy woman, drunkard, dressmaker, preacher, policeman, the webfoot cocklewomen and the tidy wives. Young girls lie bedded soft or glide in their dreams, with rings and trousseaux, bridesmaided by glow-worms down the aisles of the organplaying wood. The boys are dreaming wicked or of the bucking ranches of the night and the jollyrodgered sea. And the anthracite statues of the horses sleep in the fields, and the cows in the byres, and the dogs in the wetnosed yards; and the cats nap in the slant corners or lope sly, streaking and needling, on the one cloud of the roofs.

You can hear the dew falling, and the hushed town breathing. Only *your* eyes are unclosed to see the black and folded town fast, and slow, asleep. And you alone can hear the invisible starfall, the darkest-before-dawn minutely dewgrazed stir of the black, dab-filled sea where the *Arethusa*, the *Curlew* and the *Skylark*, *Zanzibar*, *Rhiannon*, the *Rover*, the *Cormorant*, and the *Star of Wales* tilt and ride.

Listen. It is night moving in the streets, the processional salt slow musical wind in Coronation Street and Cockle Row, it is the grass growing on Llaregyb Hill, dewfall, starfall, the sleep of birds in Milk Wood.

Listen. It is night in the chill, squat chapel, hymning in bonnet and brooch and bombazine black, butterfly choker and bootlace bow, coughing like nannygoats, sucking mintoes, fortywinking hallelujah; night in the four-ale, quiet as a domino; in Ocky Milkman's lofts like a mouse with gloves; in Dai Bread's bakery flying like black flour. It is to- night in Donkey Street, trotting silent, with seaweed on its hooves, along the cockled cobbles, past curtained fernpot, text and trinket, harmonium, holy dresser, watercolours done by hand, china dog and rosy tin teacaddy. It is night neddying among the snuggeries of babies.

Look. It is night, dumbly, royally winding through the Coronation cherry trees; going through the graveyard of Bethesda with winds gloved and folded, and dew doffed; tumbling by the Sailors Arms.

Time passes. Listen. Time passes.

From *Under Milk Wood* by Dylan Thomas.

SENTENCE STRUCTURE

Note for a start the author's use of the structure of the list —

(a) . . . limping invisible down to the sloeblack, slow, black, fishing-boat bobbing sea.

(b) . . . the babies are sleeping, the farmers, the fishers, the tradesmen and pensioners, cobbler, school-teacher, postman and publican, the undertaker and the fancy woman, drunkard, dressmaker, preacher, policeman, the webfoot cocklewomen and the tidy wives.

See if you can find another list in the extract.

What structure are these lists in — polysyndetic or asyndetic? And what is the effect of that structure? Think about what we said above about the effects of these two kinds of lists.

CONNOTATIONS

We've talked about the connotations of words and how the context guides us as to which of the connotations or word pictures are the most appropriate. Look at the beginning of the extract:

It is spring, moonless night in the small town, starless and bible-black.

Thomas uses four words to create and intensify the darkness: "moonless", "night", "starless" and "bible-black". "Bible-black" seems odd, but given that the play is set in a Welsh village which is very religious — almost repressively religious — then the connotations of "bible-black" become clearer — it's not just a colour image, but suggests the attitudes of the inhabitants. The use of the lists further intensifies the darkness and sense of foreboding.

Many of the words that Dylan Thomas uses or even makes up do not make much sense outwith the context he creates. Once we grasp the context, we can understand and appreciate the effect that he is creating by his use of the words and then we get a glimpse of the meaning:

(a) ". . . the boys are dreaming . . . of the bucking ranches of the night and the jollyrodgered sea."

"bucking" isn't normally used to describe ranches, and he has made up the word "jollyrodgered", but you can see that both words are appropriate and highly effective within the context.

(b) "And the anthracite statues of the horses sleep in the fields . . . and the dogs in the wetnosed yards."

Again the horses are not statues made of anthracite, and he has made up the compound adjective "wetnosed" — but you can see why.

Can you find any other examples such as these?

In the Parts of Speech tables on pages 14–16, I mentioned present participles: the bit of the verb that ends in -ing. Note how often Thomas uses such words in this extract: "streaking and needling", "dew falling", "hushed town breathing", "night moving" — there are many, many examples. What is the effect of all this? Present participles not only stress movement, they suggest the action is happening now — in the present — and is happening continuously. And that is exactly the effect the dramatist creates as the speaker invites the audience to listen to and look at all that is happening as dawn breaks over the village.

NARRATIVE STRUCTURE

So far we have looked at grammar and word-order, denotation and connotation, and context. What other techniques are open to a writer? We have to come back to the word "structure". Just as a writer structures a sentence in order to create a certain effect, he has also to structure the whole piece he has written. He will structure the whole novel — or short story or play or poem — he will structure chapters, paragraphs, sentences; in a play he will build acts and scenes into the structure he wants; and in poetry he will use lines, verses and / or verse-paragraphs. We'll go into this in more detail when we look more closely at the novel, drama, and poetry. Meanwhile it's enough to draw your attention to the fact that all texts — even short extracts — have a structure. The extract from *Under Milk Wood* has its own structure. It opens with a wide view of the town, sketching in a few general details. then (much as the opening of a film might do) it moves in more closely looking at intricate detail. Note the use of "Listen" and "Look" and the points at which these words come in the speech — that's also part of the structure. If I tell you that the play was originally written for radio, can you then detect anything in the structure that might make it more appropriate for radio, than for, say, television?

Candidates find the idea of structure baffling. But really it is not that difficult a concept. Think, first of all, of the structure of buildings or bridges. If I were to ask you to describe the structure of the Forth Rail Bridge, you would probably have no difficulty: you would tell me about its length, its height, the width of the deck that carries the railway line, the fact that it is constructed in cantilevers, made of iron, etcetera. You would think about length, breadth, and width.

When next you are asked about the structure of a story, then think instead in terms of time: all stories, fiction and non-fiction, poems, dramas, films are structured in time. When you think of it, that is really quite obvious. If some incident occurs in school, and you decide to tell your parents about it at night time, you structure your story in time because the event took place in time. You begin at the beginning, move on to the middle and conclude with the end. That is how all literature is structured — beginning, middle, and end. Sometimes we vary the order of the beginning and middle and produce a story which follows a middle, beginning, and end structure — and we call that *flashback*. The story begins in the middle and then flashes back to the beginning by way of explaining the events that led up to the point where it started. A perfect example of a novel which uses flashback is *Catcher in the Rye* by J.D. Salinger.

Another aspect of structure is the way in which the story is told — its narrative structure. Narrative structure is the overall structure of a story.

There are four main ways in which a story can be told. These "ways" are sometimes referred to as the point of view — and you have point of view in poems as well as in prose. Sometimes, especially within a poem, the point of view shifts, though this can be the case in a novel as well.

1. ***Omniscient Author*** — the story is told by the author who knows everything about all the characters.

2. ***First Person Narration*** — the story is told by one of the characters. The advantage of this method of narration is that the reader gets to know the character intimately, but the disadvantage is that the character telling the story has to be present at all times. The reader's information is filtered through the mind of the person narrating the story which means that the telling of the story can be biased.

3. ***Third Person Narration*** — the story is told by the author but concentrating on or through the eyes of one of the characters. The story is told in the third person but, since the author is focusing on a particular character, that character has to be present. The problem for an author is that it is tempting to shift the point of focus and thus confuse the reader.

    Sometimes the narrative is told in the second person — the *you* form. An excellent example of the use of this form can be found in *Complicity* by Iain Banks where the murderer's thoughts are conveyed in the second person, adding an immediacy and making the reader feel as though he / she were present.

4. **Stream of Consciousness** — the story is told by one of the characters but is structured in a much less conventional way than first person narration. The writer tries to capture, in a stream of consciousness novel, the actual thinking processes of a human being, thus in the narrative the reader is faced with the character's distractions, daydreams, memories, and other thoughts triggered by what he / she has seen, or is thinking about, or by a word that he / she has just used.

Stream of Consciousness is very much a twentieth century development in the novel.

Let us sum up now. The critical reader should be aware of various aspects of the novel, such as:

(a) **Theme** — the theme of a work of fiction is what it is about. Any novel or short story will explore some issue, usually of significance to the human situation, condition, or experience. The reader has to determine what the theme is for him / herself recognising that theme is established by means of the various techniques set out below.

(b) **Atmosphere / Mood / Tone** — right at the very beginning of the novel the writer has to establish an appropriate atmosphere or mood or tone.

(c) **Setting** — the writer must also establish an appropriate setting, both in time and place. Too often, we forget that time is as vital an aspect of setting as place. Not only should we be concerned with the time in which the novel is set and the time span which it covers, but also we should pay attention to when it was written since that is a dimension of time that will affect our understanding of what the novel is about.

(d) **Plot** — a series of incidents does not constitute plot. Plot must always involve causality — one incident is caused by another. Thus, as E.M. Foster illustrated in *Aspects of the Novel*, *The king died and then the queen died* is a series of incidents but not plot, whereas *The king died and then the queen died of grief* is plot. Plot will always be in a chronological sequence — *beginning > middle > end* — though sometimes we can have *middle > beginning > end*, sometimes referred to as flashback, a technique often used in films.

(e) **Characterisation** — the writer must establish the major characters for his / her story. Clearly, these characters will be developed by their interaction with each other, with the setting, and with the plot. The writer must also establish the minor characters who will be used for a variety of purposes. It is vitally important to see all characters as a product of the writer's imagination and technical skill and *not* as having a life of their own independent of the work of fiction. A *character study* can be a misleading term since it suggests that the character being studied has a life outside the work of fiction; a character study should avoid psychoanalysis and concentrate on literary technique.

(f) **Symbolism** — the writer uses symbols to represent the themes or characters or even mood. Rain, for example, can be a powerful symbol.

We have already established that *Catcher in the Rye* by J.D. Salinger uses the technique of flashback. But also the book is told in First Person Narration by the main character, Holden Caulfield — which means that the reader sees everything from Holden's point of view. All incidents and other characters are seen through his eyes, therefore the reader has to make up his / her mind about how much is Holden's opinion and how much is reality. Point of view is restricted and is that of a particularly jaundiced teenager — is his idea that everyone is a phoney acceptable? The only people he likes are those who have died or who have not yet made it to the adult world he so despises.

The book begins in the mental institution to which Holden was committed the Christmas before. He tells his story which traces the events during the four days the previous December which led to his mental deterioration and breakdown.

The last chapter of the book also refers to the institution: the book begins and ends in the same place, which gives it shape — otherwise the story could begin and end anywhere.

But before we study prose in detail, I want to say something in the next Chapter about the device of metaphor.

CHAPTER FOUR
METAPHOR

I think that one of the most important devices to understand is the device of metaphor. No doubt you have been taught almost since Primary School that metaphor is where one thing is compared to another. Let's examine the following very traditional example of a metaphor:

Kevin was a lion in the battle

Now obviously Kevin was not literally a lion: it is his behaviour which is being compared to that of a lion. Now if we are asked whether this metaphor is effective, we have first of all to establish if it is appropriate. Did Kevin fight with lion-like qualities? So, first of all we have to establish exactly what lion-like qualities are. Note — and this is important — that Kevin is being compared to a lion, but lions are not being compared to Kevin.

If we call Kevin *Term A* and lion *Term B*, we can then work out the qualities of *Term B* and see whether or not they apply to *Term A*. *Term A* is always the thing to which the comparison is being made and *Term B* is always the thing to which *Term A* is compared.

Let's demonstrate what I mean graphically:

Kevin was a lion in the battle
    | |
Term A   *Term B*

Right, now we need to establish the qualities of *Term B* — that is, what qualities do lions show when they are fighting? The answer, you tell me, is that they fight fiercely, aggressively, bravely, and violently.

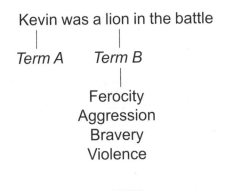

Kevin was a lion in the battle
    | |
Term A   *Term B*
             |
Ferocity
Aggression
Bravery
Violence

If Kevin actually fought with these qualities then the metaphor is appropriate and therefore effective. The only thing that you might say is that the metaphor is not really very original and is a bit of a cliché.

But, I hear you ask, what then is a simile? Isn't it a device of comparison too, only one which uses *like* or *as*? You are completely right. A simile is very like a metaphor, only weaker — the comparison is less strong.

Let us examine another metaphor which, this time, is a bit more original. Look carefully at the following line spoken by Macbeth:

Oh full of scorpions is my mind, dear wife!

Macbeth's mind is not literally full of scorpions — Shakespeare here is making a comparison between Macbeth's mind and a nest full of scorpions. Scorpions are vicious creatures whose poisonous stings are extremely painful and often fatal. Clearly, Macbeth is saying that, far from being happy and content, his mind is full of poison and pain.

But we have to ask ourselves whether or not this metaphor is effective. Macbeth is comparing his mind to scorpions — once again, let's call what is being compared (in this case his mind) *Term A* and the thing to which it is being compared (in this case scorpions) *Term B*. We can set it out as follows, though note that *Term B* appears first:

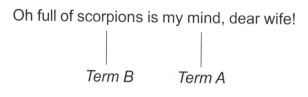

Oh full of scorpions is my mind, dear wife!

Term B   Term A

Now since *Term B* is the comparison we need to examine its connotations — in other words the connotations of scorpions. Note that we do not need to say anything about *Term A*.

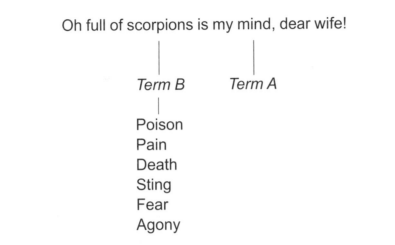

Oh full of scorpions is my mind, dear wife!

Term B   Term A

Poison
Pain
Death
Sting
Fear
Agony

The question now is whether these connotations, given the context, are appropriate. In this case the answer is yes, since Macbeth is suffering total insecurity in his ill-gotten position as king, therefore the metaphor is effective.

Metaphor is a device of comparison, where one thing is being compared to another in order to suggest a resemblance between the two things but also to illuminate the one being compared. But metaphor is more than just a figure of speech or a literary device. There is a sense in which metaphor is the basis of all literature in that a story — any story — is not only important in itself but is also important because it is a metaphor of human existence. In other words, the story — any story — invites us to make a comparison between the story itself and the comment that it makes on the nature of human existence. You can see then that literature is not just something to be mugged up for examinations but has a very rich contribution to make to our understanding of the nature of existence. That is what I mean when I say that metaphor is the basis of all literature.

I shall choose a concrete example to illustrate what I mean. Read carefully the following poem by Philip Larkin:

AFTERNOONS

Summer is fading.
The leaves fall in ones and twos
From trees bordering
The new recreation ground.
In the hollows of afternoons
Young mothers assemble
At swing and sandpit
Setting free their children.

Behind them, at intervals,
Stand husbands in skilled trades,
An estateful of washing,
And the albums, lettered
Our Wedding, lying
Near the television:
Before them, the wind
Is ruining their courting-places

That are still courting-places
(But the lovers are all in school),
And their children, so intent on
Finding more unripe acorns,
Expect to be taken home.
Their beauty has thickened.
Something is pushing them
To the side of their own lives.

The poem is about the dull, stultifying, routine nature of women's lives —
especially the lives of those women who have given up work in order to look after
young children. The poem is full of metaphors — images which Larkin composes
and with which we, as readers, make comparisons. For example:

Summer is fading.
The leaves fall in ones and twos
From trees bordering
The new recreation ground.

Now summer could, quite literally, be fading: the poem, we can argue, is set at the end of summer and the leaves are just beginning — slowly — to fall from the trees. But given the context that I have suggested above, this image of summer fading is also metaphorical — it invites a comparison between the idea of summer fading and the idea that this is a stage in women's lives. Let me explain: if we take the seasons as stages in all our lives, then spring is equivalent to youth, summer is equivalent to young adulthood, autumn to encroaching age, and winter to old age and death. The women, then, are at the end of summer — they are reaching the end of the best time in their lives and are approaching middle age. But Larkin develops this image further when he adds that the leaves are falling in ones and twos, thus suggesting that although the ageing process may be slow, nevertheless it has begun. There is also the suggestion that as this ageing process progresses so does their loss of beauty.

In this case, *Term A* is implied — the women about whom Larkin is writing. We realise this from the context of the whole poem. At least, we realise given the context of the entire poem that the first line can be taken metaphorically as well as literally. Larkin is presenting us with an image — of summer fading — which is both literal and metaphorical.

We can, then, analyse the first line thus:

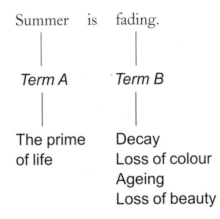

If you go through the process that I have outlined above the business of commenting on the effectiveness of a metaphor becomes easy. In *Afternoons*, there are many metaphors — images which Larkin presents in such a way that we, as readers, can make comparisons with the lives of the women, and by making the comparison we see that the lives of these women are made clearer and the theme of the poem better illustrated.

Let's look at the whole of the second stanza:

> Behind them, at intervals,
> Stand husbands in skilled trades,
> An estateful of washing,
> And the albums, lettered
> *Our Wedding*, lying
> Near the television:
> Before them, the wind
> Is ruining their courting-places

The husbands in skilled trades are not *literally* standing behind the women: the word here a metaphorical meaning of supporting the women — financially, emotionally, psychologically? The image of the wedding album lying near the television set is also interesting in that it suggests that television has taken over the centre of their lives and the wedding album is now of secondary importance. The notion of the wind ruining their courting places is also metaphorical in that *the wind* suggests a force (the boring, stultifying, routine nature of their existence) that will destroy the romantic, spontaneous, fun-loving notions that we associate with a young couple in love suggested by *courting-places*.

I have used the term *image* quite frequently. What exactly do we mean by the word *image*? As with so many terms in English criticism, it is one which is easy enough to identify but more difficult to define. We all think we know what an image is — it is a kind of mental picture, you may tell me. And that would be right, but images can also involve senses which are not necessarily visual. Orwell, in his essay *Shooting an Elephant*, when describing the effect of shooting the elephant uses an interesting simile

> The thick blood welled out of him like red velvet

Here the image is visual — you can "picture" the blood oozing from the elephant — but it is also a tactile image, one which appeals to our sense of touch. The word "velvet" suggests richness, smoothness, heaviness — all of which are images to do with touch rather than sight.

Images — and imagery — then can appeal to any of our five senses:

Visual images	Appeal to our sense of sight
Tactile images	Appeal to our sense of touch
Auditory images	Appeal to our sense of hearing
Olfactory images	Appeal to our sense of smell
Taste images	Appeal to our sense of taste

You do not have to know these terms, but you do need to be aware that images can appeal to more than just our sense of sight.

Many images, then, can be metaphorical — the writer is using the image metaphorically, creating a comparison between what ever he is talking about and the subject of the image in order for the image to illuminate his subject matter.

METONYMY

There is then a strong link between imagery and metaphor and, indeed, I can claim that all metaphors involve images, but I cannot claim that all images are metaphors. That is because some images are not used in order to create comparisons but are used, rather, as representations.

Let me explain.

As well as needing to know about metaphor, you also need to know about metonymy. Whereas metaphor is a device of comparison, metonymy is a device of representation. Sometimes we use an image not to invite a comparison but to represent the attributes, values or qualities of the thing we attribute talking about.

Let's take a simple example.

Many of you will choose to wear clothes which sport labels — Adidas, Nike, Stone Island. All of these companies have an easily recognised logo or emblem which is displayed on the garments. Now these logos or emblems are there not just to advertise the company in question, but to represent the values, qualities or attributes of the company. Not only that, but just as, say, the Nike label represents the image of Nike, the fact that you have chosen to wear it says something about your image as well — the image you want to portray to others and by which you want to be recognised. The symbol or logo, then, represents a great deal!

It is very important to understand the nature of metonymy. It isn't just some abstract concept or literary device thought up to torment candidates. A measure of its importance has to be the millions of pounds spent by companies in designing and presenting their logos, emblems or brand images. Both First Bus and Stagecoach have fairly recently rebranded themselves at an enormous cost, simply because these companies recognise the power of a corporate brand image by which the public will not only recognise the product but will associate the logo with the values and qualities of the company concerned. Think of BP, Esso, Sainsbury's, Asda, Applemac, Sony, Microsoft, Scotrail, Easyjet, and I am positive that you can immediately think of their various logos, all of which are metonymic devices representing the values and qualities of the respective companies.

Advertising, television, newspaper and billboard, are perfect visual and print media by which companies can portray their logos. Next time you are watching a commercial television channel or reading a newspaper or passing a billboard look out for the metonymic devices!

The logo or emblem is, then, a symbol that says something about the company that sports it and, in the case of designer clothes, says something about you, the person who is wearing it. The logo is a metonymic device because it represents something larger, more significant, than itself.

Images can then be metonymic. The image of a rose, for example, can be metonymic in that the rose can be used to represent love, and often is in poetry. What I am saying is that when the image is really symbolic, then the device being used is metonymy — the symbol is being used to represent something greater or more significant than itself. When you think about it, a country's flag is an excellent example of metonymy. The Union Jack, for example, represents the values, qualities, and culture of Britain and all things British. Someone wearing Union Jack underpants, on the other hand, is a metonymic device representing values of a quite different type!

A comment in passing. We have tended to associate literary criticism or textual analysis as a method of examining *literary* texts. But what is really interesting is that *all* texts — newspaper, television, radio, billboard advertisements, company logos / brand images, any printed or visual or auditory text can be subjected to careful analysis. Next time you go out in your Versace top, Diesel jeans, and Nike trainers, just think of the number of texts you are displaying — every one a metonymic device. Including yourself!

But this book is about literature and not media. We are examining the use of metonymy in literary works: prose, drama, and poetry. Look again at the third verse of *Afternoons*:

> And their children, so intent on
> Finding more unripe acorns,
> Expect to be taken home.

Now the image of children being intent on finding more unripe acorns is metonymic. There is no comparison being made. we have to assume that the children are actually looking for acorns, but the image of *unripe acorns* is metonymic in that acorns represent seeds from which great oaks grow. In other words, the image suggests something greater than itself, the notion of children looking for greater things to come!

Let's take another example — an extract from an Isaac Rosenberg war poem, *Break of Day in the Trenches*, and you will see what I mean. The poet is in the trenches as day breaks and he comments on a rat which has leapt over his hand:

> Droll rat, they would shoot you if they knew
> Your cosmopolitan sympathies.
> Now you have touched this English hand
> You will do the same to a German
> Soon, no doubt, if it be your pleasure
> To cross the sleeping green between.
> It seems you inwardly grin as you pass
> Strong eyes, fine limbs, haughty athletes,
> Less chanced than you for life,
> Bonds to the whims of murder,
> Sprawled the bowels of the earth,
> The torn fields of France.

Now here the image of the rat is not metaphorical — he isn't comparing rat-like qualities with the war or anything else for that matter. The rat is used to symbolise the cosmopolitan nature of war — he is making the point that the horror of war touches everybody, German and British alike. But look at the number of metonymic devices he uses here — "sleeping green", "strong eyes, fine limbs, haughty athletes" — all representing aspects of how he feels about the war. Let's look more closely at those lines:

> It seems you inwardly grin as you pass
> Strong eyes, fine limbs, haughty athletes,
> Less chanced than you for life,

Here the rat represents not so much a disgusting creature as a symbol of impartiality. He gives it anthropomorphic (ascribing to animals characteristics that are purely human) qualities: the idea of the rat grinning continues his earlier claim that it is a "sardonic" rat. It is amused by the irony that these fit and handsome young men are about to die in a horrible and undignified way. Even the lowly rat has more chance of life than these men. Rosenberg continues to use the device of the rat almost throughout the poem. He comments on the rat's grinning attitude as it passes the young men, and he also addresses the rat directly later in the poem when he writes:

> What do you see in our eyes
> At the shrieking iron and flame
> Hurled through still heavens?

The point is that in the rat he finds a creature at the opposite end of the scale from human beings, yet he ascribes it qualities of understanding that the more developed human beings are incapable of — if they were they would not be involved in this horrific war. Again, "iron" and "flame" are metonymic representations of the war itself.

The very powerful image:

> The torn fields of France.

is effective in that the alliteration draws attention to the words themselves and thereby to the metonymic nature of the image, an image which powerfully represents the war and its effects not only in terms of the fields themselves, but of France and ultimately the whole of Europe. The "torn fields", then, represent the entire arena of war.

But let's return to the image of the rose for a little while. Imagine you are in the cinema and one scene in the film involves a close up of a single red rose. What you see in huge wide screen dimension and glorious Technicolor is, obviously, not a real rose. It is a representation of a rose produced by a strong light being projected through celluloid and, as such, must be a metonymic device. But within the context of the film, the close-up of the rose is also metonymic in that the image is being used to represent a dramatic (because of the close-up) indication of love (because of the red rose).

Drama also exploits the device of metonymy. For example, as Macbeth makes his murderous way in the middle of the night to the sleeping Duncan, he sees a dagger before him. The dagger, of course, does not exist; it is a figment of his overwrought imagination, but the fact that he thinks he sees it causes him to pause and reflect on the nature of the deed that he is about to perform. The vision of the dagger is metonymic: it represents the means by which he is to kill Duncan, the murder itself, the temptation and desire to become king, threat, and the fact that he can't quite grasp it may represent also the elusiveness of success.

Whatever play you are studying for your course, think about the symbolic elements used by the author to help portray situation, theme, characters, plot, mood. The audience recognises the metonymic effect, and that in itself brings about a deeper understanding of the play itself.

This has been a complex chapter but it can, perhaps, be summed up thus: metaphor is a device of comparison whereas metonymy is a device of representation. Both are important literary devices; a full understanding of them will help enormously in understanding how literature works. Look for the image and then ask yourself how the image is being used — as metaphor or as metonymy. Then you can evaluate the effect.

CHAPTER FIVE

PROSE

Of all the genres in literature, prose is perhaps unique. Drama is something which is performed and requires actors and an audience; poetry, too, is often performed, and benefits from being read aloud and followed by a group discussion; but prose, particularly the novel, is entirely a private experience. The reader enters imaginatively and therefore privately into the world of the novel, recreating all that has been set before him or her by the novelist. Another aspect of the novel that makes it different is the sheer size of it: a play lasts for no more than two and a half hours, a poem can take only a few minutes to read, and each is often experienced at one sitting, so to speak. But the novel can take several days to read, has to be picked up and put down, and can, consequently, be difficult to "contain" in the imagination. That also makes it difficult to teach and even more difficult to study: which is why teachers often break up the novel into constituent elements such as "plot", "characterisation", "setting", etcetera.

But first a word about the word "prose". You know what a page of drama looks like with characters on the left, stage instructions in italics and in brackets, the words spoken set out as dialogue; poetry is written in lines and verses. But prose is almost devoid of any of these conventions: it is written in blocks of print where line endings are of no importance and which contain words which may or may not be spoken. If the words are spoken they are punctuated by direct speech marks called *inverted commas.* Prose can be the text book you are using in geography, mathematics or science, the newspaper or magazine you read on the bus, the essay you are studying in English. It can also be the novel you have currently taken out from the library. In other words, prose can be either prose non-fiction or prose fiction. Prose fiction concerns any prose work which is imaginatively written, which creates a world that does not exist (though it may be based on one which does) and which involves characters which aren't real, but are "made up". Prose non-fiction concerns the real world or the world of facts; it may be a piece recalling events which have occurred; or it may be a reflective piece where the author gives his opinion on events or people or places. Perhaps the easiest way to remember the difference is to bear in mind that novels and short stories are *fiction*, whereas essays, pieces of journalism, travel books are *non-fiction*.

We shall begin with fiction, particularly the novel. Your literature course will contain a study of one or more novels, and the question which will spring to your mind is: "What is the best way of tackling the text?" As always, go back to the first of the three questions set out at the beginning of this book — *(a)* What is the text about? — the answer to which, as you know, provides you with the theme or themes. I know that this isn't an easy task — you need to spend quite a bit of time thinking out what the issues in the novel are for you. Once you've done that and written down the themes, you need to go back to the text to see how the themes are established, which scenes (or incidents) illustrate these themes, and what part the characters play in the development of them.

I would like you to take time to read *The Power and The Glory* by Graham Greene: there is bound to be a copy in your school or college or library. It is, I think, one of the major novels of last century, and though it may appear difficult it is worth the bother. It is ostensibly a thriller, but it does get to the heart of many of the concerns of the 20th century and does make clear the two main ways of looking at human beings and their nature. One of its major themes is the conflict between militaristic atheism and corrupt Christianity — the conflict between those who want to achieve a perfect society here on earth by eradicating free will and those who accept that because human beings have free will they can make corrupt choices but that perfection will come in the next life. That theme is established in a number of ways, not least by the use of two characters — the unnamed Lieutenant and the Whisky Priest who are each symbolic of the two forces involved. But what is really fascinating is the way in which Greene introduces the reader to these characters: the Whisky Priest in Chapter I is seen as seedy, shabby, alcoholic, corrupt — but his compassion prevents him from escaping from communist Mexico; the Lieutenant, on the other hand, is cold, efficient, desperate to introduce to his State the ideas of equality, fraternity, justice — but he lacks compassion. The Lieutenant is "the little dapper figure of hate carrying his secret of love". He is constantly compared to a priest — "something priest-like", "his monastic cell", his desire to teach the little children — and the priest is the one whose flesh is weak. You should trace these ideas as you read the text. There are other themes in this complex novel, too, of course — and you should try to think them out for yourself.

Think of the novel you are presently studying in your course. What are its themes? How does the setting, characterisation, plot help establish and develop those themes? —

But perhaps most fundamental of all is the structure of the novel. I said that *The Power and the Glory* is a thriller — and that is how Greene has structured his story. He uses the chase, where the Lieutenant has to chase, find and execute the Whisky Priest since the Lieutenant's state cannot tolerate any form of religion. How has the novel that you have been studying been structured? How has it been put together by the novelist? What setting has been chosen, when has it been set and over what period of time? What role does time play in the development of the plot? What is the relationship between the setting and the plot, and between setting and character? But, as well as that, you need to study how the novel has been built up — what are the key scenes? How do they advance the plot? How do they affect the outcome? How do they contribute to character and to theme?

In *The Power and The Glory*, the key central scene must be the one in jail where the Whisky Priest, having been captured without being recognised, is thrown into a cell where he comes upon all of humanity: the prison cell is the microcosm of the world. The contrast is also made between himself, with his alcoholism, illegitimate child, and his state of mortal sin, and another character — the pious woman, with her state of grace but also with her martyrish outlook and utter self-righteousness. At the end of the scene the Whisky Priest comes face to face with the Lieutenant for the second time, and for the second time the Lieutenant fails to recognise him. Obviously, there is a great deal more to the scene than that, but it fulfils several functions — it allows Greene an opportunity to make several observations about human attitudes and to comment incisively on the hypocrisy of certain religious people's views. It also builds up the tension in this thriller chase by the lieutenant and the priest meeting but the former failing to capture the latter, ironically since the priest has just been released from jail.

When we read a novel we can stop at a particular bit we like and think about it. It may be a point at which a character is introduced or where two characters are in conflict or where the writer seems to halt the narrative in order to comment. Or it may, quite simply, be a piece of description which sets a scene or symbolises some aspect of the plot and / or theme. The point is that we can savour such a "moment" in a way in which we can't while watching a film or play. We can think of such a scene in terms of itself, in terms of its immediate context and in terms of the novel as a whole. Indeed, such a task is no bad practice for your critical essay question, since often a question asks you to discuss the role of such a scene.

As I said, people have often asked me how to study a novel. The answer is to be formal and rigorous by using an assignment sheet. Your answers to the following assignment sheet will provide you with your own notes for revision.

NOVEL ASSIGNMENT SHEET

(a) Who tells the story? (Chief character in the first person / minor character in the first person / author in the third person / any other means.)

(b) What are the advantages of the chosen method of telling the story?

(c) What is the point of view in the novel — restricted to one character or does it shift between characters or does it involve all characters — and what is the effect of that point of view?

(d) What type of novel is it? (Fantasy, thriller, science fiction, crime, etcetera.)

(e) Name the main characters, and the minor ones.

(f) What is the nature of conflict in the novel?

(g) Is the chief / main character involved in any kind of internal conflict?

(h) What is the outcome of the conflict and how is it arrived at?

(i) What are the themes of the novel? (Jealousy, ambition, envy, revenge, unrequited love, duplicity, ingratitude, etcetera.)

(j) How are these themes established / developed / illustrated? (Think in terms of characters, scenes, plot, setting.)

(k) How well does the beginning of the novel — the opening chapter / pages — introduce us to plot, setting, character, theme, etcetera?

(l) What expectation does the opening set up in the reader?

(m) How well does the ending resolve the issues and how satisfactorily does it meet the expectations already set up in us?

(n) Did you genuinely enjoy the novel? Why? Pick out one or two aspects you especially enjoyed.

(o) What do you feel you learned from studying the novel?

SHORT STORY

The short story is also part of prose fiction. Familiarity with a short story must include familiarity with the form of the short story, and more nonsense is perhaps written about the short story form than about any other aspect of literature. Candidates still trot out the importance of the "twist in the tail" when some of the best short stories display no such quirk. What distinguishes the short story from the novel is its "single-mindedness": it invariably concerns itself with one idea, and all that the short story contains — language, setting, characterisation, atmosphere — is geared to the deployment of that idea. It also tends to have a restricted point of view. What characterises the short story is its economy: nothing is wasted, nothing is extra, everything counts, everything is pared down to the bare essentials. And it all goes towards what it is the author wants to say, to depict, to illustrate. Everything is focused very sharply, in contrast with the novel, which by its nature is more diffuse, more wide-ranging.

If you are going to study a short story for the exam, then make sure that it isn't all you do for the prose section (there might not be a question that allows for the short story) and make sure you know it and understand it thoroughly in terms of its form.

NON-FICTION

But, of course, prose includes non-fiction as well as novels and short stories. "Non-fiction" is a term which covers a great many kinds of books: travel books, biographies, autobiographies, essays and journalism. We read non-fiction because we want to learn something, whereas with fiction what we learn is almost by-the-way. When you study non-fiction then you must begin from that standpoint: what is it I have learned from this book or this essay or this piece of journalism?

But learning from a piece of writing means re-examining our "received ideas". All of us, as we grow up, develop what are called "received ideas" — attitudes and ways of thinking that we absorb quite uncritically from our parents, friends, immediate social environment, the press, television, our culture at large. Often our political outlook isn't something we have thought out for ourselves but is an expression of a whole set of beliefs we have somehow accepted without ever having thought about them, far less having challenged them. But it is not just in the area of politics — though by "politics" I mean really our beliefs about what human nature is like — that we have "received ideas": we have received ideas about authority, work, people of other races, people of other religions, foreigners, minority groups, women, men, marriage, friendship . . . the list is endless. The essay and some journalistic pieces can sometimes be the first real challenge we come across to our received notions. Non-fiction is usually written to convey and explore ideas and in so doing enables us, the readers, to examine our own ideas and to see the flaws, weaknesses and, often, prejudices that run through them. We see our ideas in a fresh light; we can begin to challenge our ways of looking at things with an intellectual rigour that is as rewarding as it is illuminating.

Your study of non-fiction, then, has to be open-minded. Concentrate not just on what you have learned from the piece, but on how you have been challenged, how your ideas have altered as a result of having read it.

The next stage is to examine carefully how — the ways in which — the author presents his argument. The role of narrative (and by "narrative" I mean "the story") is less important in non-fiction, but is nevertheless still present. In *Shooting an Elephant* by George Orwell, for example, the narrative is really quite an important element in conveying what it is he wants to say. The essay is about (among other things) the nature of authority and how the authority figure is not free to be authoritarian but has to act in a way in which those over whom he has "power" expect him to act. To make this point he tells the story of the time he had to shoot an elephant. The narrative is the vehicle that carries the theme. (Narrative should not be confused with plot: *narrative* is the retelling of events in their time-sequence, whereas *plot* is the deliberate construction of events with some notion of explanation or cause. The traditional example will serve: as we have already seen, "The King died and then the Queen died" is narrative, whereas "The King died and then the Queen died of grief" is plot.)

You should also concentrate on the language features of the piece of non-fiction you are studying as well as tile structure. Look carefully at the following extract from *Shooting an Elephant* where Orwell describes the death of the elephant:

The crowd grew very still, and a deep, low, happy sigh, as of people who see the theatre curtain go up at last, breathed from innumerable throats. They were going to have their bit of fun after all. The rifle was a beautiful German thing with cross-hair sights. I did not then know that in shooting an elephant one would shoot to cut an imaginary bar running from ear-hole to ear-hole. I ought, therefore, as the elephant was sideways on, to have aimed straight at his ear-hole; actually I aimed several inches in front of this, thinking the brain would be further forward.

When I pulled the trigger I did not hear the bang or feel the kick — one never does when a shot goes home — but I heard the devilish roar of glee that went up from the crowd. In that instant, in too short a time, one would have thought, even for the bullet to get there, a mysterious, terrible change had come over the elephant. He neither stirred nor fell, but every line of his body had altered. He looked suddenly stricken, shrunken, immensely old, as though the frightful impact of the bullet had paralysed him without knocking him down. At last, after what seemed a long time — it might have been five seconds, I dare say — he sagged flabbily to his knees. His mouth slobbered. An enormous senility seemed to have settled upon him. One could have imagined him thousands of years old. I fired again into the same spot. At the second shot he did not collapse but climbed with desperate slowness to his feet and stood weakly upright, with legs sagging and head drooping. I fired a third time. That was the shot that did for him. You could see the agony of it jolt his whole body and knock the last remnant of strength from his legs. But in falling he seemed for a moment to rise, for as his hind legs collapsed beneath him he seemed to tower upwards like a huge rock toppling, his trunk reaching skywards like a tree. He trumpeted, for the first and only time. And then down he came, his belly towards me, with a crash that seemed to shake the ground even where I lay.

I got up. The Burmans were already racing past me across the mud. It was obvious that the elephant would never rise again, but he was not dead. He was breathing very rhythmically with long rattling gasps, his great mound of side painfully rising and falling. His mouth was wide open — I could see far down into caverns of pale pink throat. I waited a long time for him to die, but his breathing did not weaken. Finally I fired my two remaining shots into the spot where I thought his heart must be. The thick blood welled out of him like red velvet, but still he did not die. His body did not even jerk when the shots hit him, the tortured breathing continued without a pause. He was dying, very slowly and in great agony, but in some world remote from me where not even a bullet could damage him further. I felt that I had got to put an end to that dreadful noise. It seemed dreadful to see the great beast lying there, powerless to move and yet powerless to die, and not even to be able to finish him. I sent back for my small rifle and poured shot after shot into his heart and down his throat. They seemed to make no impression. The tortured gasps continued as steadily as the ticking of a clock.

In the end I could not stand it any longer and went away. I heard later that it took him half an hour to die. Burmans were bringing dahs and baskets even before I left, and I was told they had stripped his body almost to the bones by the afternoon.

From *Shooting an Elephant* by George Orwell.

What comes across most clearly is the genuineness of the writing. You know instinctively that it seems to be based on experience. The parenthesis "— one never does when a shot goes home —" reinforces the realism. But what is remarkable is the absence of cliché. The writing is fresh and vivid: "a mysterious, terrible change had come over the elephant", "He looked suddenly stricken, shrunken, immensely old", "he sagged flabbily to his knees", "caverns of pale pink throat" and so on. Orwell is the master of direct, economical language: "That was the shot that did for him.", "I got up." — simple, short, but effective sentences. Some of his images are very unusual: his breathing was in "long rattling gasps". Look how effective "rattling" is (a word we would normally associate with iron vibrating) when associated with gasps. The gasps are also described as continuing "as steadily as the ticking of a clock". I could go on.

This piece of description is essential to the theme he is conveying, because it convinces the reader that this piece of reportage is both accurate and real; it makes the reader feel as though he / she is there as an eye-witness too.

Finally, I want to mention rhythm, a word normally associated with poetry. But prose has rhythm too, and Orwell is an author who can exploit rhythm for its dramatic effect. Look at the ending of *Shooting an Elephant*.

> The older men said I was right, the younger men said it was a damn shame to shoot an elephant for killing a coolie, because an elephant was worth more than any damn Coringhee coolie. And afterwards I was very glad that the coolie had been killed; it put me legally in the right and it gave me sufficient pretext for shooting the elephant. I often wondered whether any of the others grasped that I had done it solely to avoid looking a fool.

Look at the first sentence: the parallel structure of "the older men said . . , the younger men said . . ."; the repetition of coolie and elephant; the repetition of "damn" with its shift from describing "shame" to "coolie". The rhythm of the sentence captures the language, utterances and attitudes of the two generations. But what I admire is the dramatic effect of the final sentence; the climax is "to avoid looking a fool" but examine how he delays the climax by putting it right at the end of the sentence, and even the insertion of "solely" helps delay it further.

I have used *Shooting an Elephant* as an example. The technique, however, applies to any prose work you are studying.

Finally, we need to refer again to *The Power and the Glory*. I want to look closely at the beginning of the novel partly because it is important to be able to read a text closely, partly because it is important to examine how an author establishes theme and atmosphere and partly because the kind of analysis you will be expected to perform in the Textual Analysis question, though such an analysis is useful for the Critical Essay as well.

CHAPTER 1

The Port

MR TENCH went out to look for his ether cylinder, into the blazing Mexican sun and the bleaching dust. A few vultures looked down from the roof with shabby indifference: he wasn't carrion yet. A faint feeling of rebellion stirred in Mr Tench's heart, and he wrenched up a piece of the road with splintering finger-nails and tossed it feebly towards them. One rose and flapped across the town: over the tiny plaza over the bust of an ex-president, ex-general, ex-human being, over the two stalls which sold mineral water, towards the river and the sea. It wouldn't find anything there: the sharks looked after the carrion on that side. Mr Tench went on across the plaza.

He said 'Buenos días' to a man with a gun who sat in a small patch of shade against a wall. But it wasn't like England: the man said nothing at all, just stared malevolently up at Mr Tench, as if he had never had any dealings with the foreigner, as if Mr Tench were not responsible for his two gold bicuspid teeth. Mr Tench went sweating by, past the Treasury which once had been a church, towards the quay. Half-way across he suddenly forgot what he had come out for — a glass of mineral water? That was all there was to drink in this prohibition state — except beer, but that was a government monopoly and too expensive except on special occasions. An awful feeling of nausea gripped Mr Tench in the stomach — it couldn't have been mineral water he wanted. Of course his ether cylinder. . . the boat was in. He had heard its exultant piping while he lay on his bed after lunch. He passed the barber.' and two dentists and came out between a warehouse and the customs on to the river bank.

From *The Power and the Glory* by Graham Greene

Every line, every word of this novel is chosen with deliberate care for the right effect. The very first two words of the novel are "Mr Tench": ask yourself about the sound of the word "Tench" — what does it sound like? Remind you of? Stench? Tension? What other word does it suggest? Tench — the fish. An unpleasant scavenger. But look carefully at the whole of the sentence. Mr Tench goes out to look for his ether cylinder and all that it suggests about anaesthetising feelings and pain. And when he goes out, it is into the "'blazing sun" and "bleaching dust" — the sun, normally associated with life and life-giving forces, is here associated with Hell ("blazing") and death ("bleaching dust"). "Bleaching dust" also conjures up the picture of bones lying whitened by the sun slowly becoming ashes: "ashes to ashes, dust to dust". You'll note we move from "bleaching dust" to "vultures" — ugly scavengers which live off death; the vultures look with "shabby indifference" but ignore Tench because he isn't yet "carrion". He throws a piece of the road at them and one flaps across the town. The reader follows its flight over the "bust of an ex-president, ex-general, ex-human being? (note the list in climactic structure, the repetition of "ex", the irony of "human being"), over the two stalls which sold mineral water (no alcohol in this puritanical state), out over the river towards the sea. The river and the sea represent escape from this fascist state, but we find the sea is full of sharks which "look after the carrion on that side" — in other words there is no escape. The gun is a symbol which runs through this novel, a symbol to which we are introduced in paragraph two. Mr Tench says "'Buenos días' to a man with a gun" as he walks across the plaza, past "the Treasury which had once been a church" and here we have echoes of the temple which had been taken over by the moneylenders whom Christ eventually expelled.

Therefore, right at the beginning of the novel, Greene establishes the run-down stultifying, death-ridden nature of the Mexican State from which there is no escape, except through death itself. In other words a writer with this kind of skill can establish both atmosphere and one of the major themes of his novel in two short paragraphs.

The kind of approach I have taken above is the kind of approach required for Textual Analysis, but it also involves the kind of thinking that is required for preparation for the Critical Essay.

But I need to add a word of warning. Although I have talked about Textual Analysis and the Critical Essay in the same sentence, they are in fact different kinds of questions. The Critical Essay will ask you to look at the novel (or short story or non-fiction prose) as a whole — you need to know about the themes and the techniques by which the author engages those themes. In other words, you do not want to get involved in too much detail, though your preparation for the Critical Essay may require some detailed examination of the texts. I have seen far too many candidates get so bogged down in detail in their Critical Essay questions that the marker is left guessing if the candidate has any clue what the novel is actually about. And the same advice goes for your Specialist Study Literature response: do not provide a textual analysis of the novel — or whatever — but do keep well in your sights the theme of the book about which you are writing. Then you can write about the various literary and linguistic techniques by which the author establishes and develops that theme.

CHAPTER SIX

POETRY

The study of poetry worries, frets, and quite often bores candidates. And the rich irony is that candidates who tackle poetry — both in the Critical Essay and in their Specialist Study — invariably do very well. You should not be afraid of poetry. It has to be approached in the same way as you approach prose — establish the theme and then look at the techniques by which that theme has been established and developed.

The following example will show you what I mean. Read carefully *The Castle* by Edwin Muir:

THE CASTLE

All through that summer at ease we lay,
And daily from the turret wall
We watched the mowers in the hay
And the enemy half a mile away.
They seemed no threat to us at all.

For what, we thought, had we to fear
With our arms and provender, load on load,
Our towering battlements, tier on tier,
And friendly allies drawing near
On every leafy summer road.

Our gates were strong, our walls were thick,
So smooth and high, no man could win
A foothold there, no clever trick
Could take us, have us dead or quick.
Only a bird could have got in.

What could they offer us for bait?
Our captain was brave and we were true . . .
There was a little private gate,
A little wicked wicket gate.
The wizened warder let them through.

Oh then our maze of tunnelled stone
Grew thin as treacherous as air.
The cause was lost without a groan,
The famous citadel overthrown,
And all its secret galleries bare.

How can this shameful tale be told?
I will maintain until my death
We could do nothing, being sold;
Our only enemy was gold,
And we had no arms to fight it with.

From *The Collected Poems* of Edwin Muir

Begin — as always — with the three questions

(a) What is the poem about?

(b) What effect does it have on me?

(c) How have these effects been achieved?

The answer to question *(a)*, remember, is in terms of theme — what are the themes of *The Castle*? What springs to my mind is greed, the ability of an individual or a society to be corrupted by the desire for wealth. The poet spends the first three stanzas informing us about secure their establishment is: they have strong defences and ample provisions:

> For what, we thought, had we to fear
> With our arms and provender, load on load,
> Our towering battlements, tier on tier,

The expression "we thought" suggests that this is being told retrospectively and with some regret. They also, he assures us, have plenty of friends:

> And friendly allies drawing near

But, just as we all feel that wonderful sense of security, the poet surprises us in the next stanza by revealing that all was easily lost:

> What could they offer us for bait?
> Our captain was brave and we were true . . .
> There was a little private gate,
> A little wicked wicket gate.
> The wizened warder let them through.

The second line suggests that they are unassailable and impregnable, then we realise that through one person, by means of an entrance they hadn't bothered to secure, all was lost. We can be corrupted when least expecting it by a means that is as effective as it is surprising.

But what of question *(b)*, what of the effect? In this poem, I find that sound plays a major part in the effect for me. Before I talk about sound in this poem I need to tell you something about sound generally.

First of all we need to know about vowel sounds and they effect they can have. In English there are five vowels: a, e, i, o and u. These vowels can be either *short* or *long*. For example:

short	*a*	pronounced as in *hat*
long	*a*	pronounced as in *hate*
short	*e*	pronounced as in *pet*
long	*e*	pronounced as in *Pete*
short	*i*	pronounced as in *lit*
long	*i*	pronounced as in *light*
short	*o*	pronounced as in *dot*
long	*o*	pronounced as in *dote*

The repetition of a vowel sound is called *assonance*.

But there is more to it than that. The other letters are known as consonants and can be grouped into types of sounds as follows:

Letter	*Type of Sound*	*Sound Effect*
b and p	Plosive	hard
hard c, g, qu and k	Guttural	harsh, often unpleasant
d and t	Dental	neutral
f, th and v	Fricative	can be unpleasant when combined with a short vowel
l, w and y	Liquid	mellifluous and pleasant, but the *w* sound can be mean
m and n	Nasal	usually pleasant
soft c, s, and z	Sibilant	soporific or hissing
R	Rolling	almost like a vowel

It is the combination of the consonant and the vowel sound that creates the effect. For example, it is no accident that our most effective (unpleasant) swearing words begin with the plosive *b* followed by a short vowel sound. Good taste prevents me from giving you an example, but if you are about to hammer a nail home, and, instead of hitting the nail, you hit your thumb, I am willing to wager that you will automatically form the *b* sound with your lips, as in "Oh, ya b . . .!"

I have always thought that the nastiest of the four letters words isn't a swearing word at all, but is the word *work* pronounced with a strong Scottish accent: the *w* is tightly formed by drawing the lips together to form the meanest shape you can imagine and then the vowel is pronounced with a harsh guttural *u* — *"Ye need to wurk, laddie, and wurk hard!"*

Which brings me back to the poem. Look again at the fourth stanza:

> What could they offer us for bait?
> Our captain was brave and we were true . . .
> There was a little private gate,
> A little wicked wicket gate.
> The wizened warder let them through.

and examine carefully the last two lines. Note that here we have a repetition of the *w* sound, creating the meanness that I talked about, and the *w* is followed by short vowel sounds creating a powerfully unpleasant effect. You have the words *wicked* and *wicket*, which are almost a repetition, thus drawing attention to them both and these words are followed by *wizened* and *warder*, maintaining the mean *w* sound along with the short vowel sounds. The long vowel sounds in the line before

> Our captain was brave and we were true.

help to produce the safe, secure, unassailable tone, which means that the sudden change in sound to the short, mean, ugly tone of:

> There was a little private gate,
> A little wicked wicket gate.
> The wizened warder let them through.

takes us as much by surprise as the person relating the story.

Now rhythm is very much related to the sound of the words chosen. The sound of a word depends on the vowel sounds and the consonants.

Short vowel sounds tend to be said quickly and long vowel sounds slowly. Certain consonants also create speed — for example *t* and *d*; some can create violent sounds — for example *b p*; others may slow words down — *w l m n y*; others may suggest a hissing sound which can be used in a variety of ways — *s z*.

Let's look at the opening stanza of *The Castle*:

> All through that summer at ease we lay,
> And daily from the turret wall
> We watched the mowers in the hay
> And the enemy half a mile away.
> They seemed no threat to us at all.

Note the number of long vowel sounds: "through", "ease", "lay", "daily", "mowers", "hay", "mile", "away", "seemed". Note also the consonants that slow words down: the double *ll* in *all*, the *s* and *m* of *summer*, the *s* of *ease*, the *l* of *lay*. the *l* and *y* of *daily*, the double *ll* of *wall*. the *w* of *we* and *watched*; even getting the tongue round the *t*, *ch* and *d* of *watched* helps to slow down the pace.

Now when you examine what the author is actually saying, you can see how the long, slow moving sentence contributes to those feelings of languor and security. The last line speeds up considerably (short vowel sounds and fast-sounding consonants) and, combined with the word "seemed" gives the suggestion that the security is perhaps false.

We can say a great deal about rhythm and sound and its contribution to meaning. That isn't quite right: I've been suggesting that sound *contributes* to meaning, as though somehow the two are separate — not so, sound is part of the meaning. However, you can see from the long / short distribution in the fourth stanza that the first two lines are made up of long vowel sounds and the next three of short vowel sounds. You can see why: the first two are the culmination of the security built up at the beginning of the poem, whereas the lines after the three dots suddenly and effectively expose the security for what it was — false.

In the passing; it is worth commenting on the structure of this fourth stanza. The first two lines form the climax of the build-up of to the idea of everything being secure — the first line is a question which implies its own answer (we call that a *rhetorical question*) and the second makes a statement that is almost a cliché: captains are always brave and the troops are always true. The interesting point is the use of the three dots after "true. . . ." We call the device of three dots at the end of a sentence *aposiopesis* and they suggest either something unfinished or a change in direction. We read the next three lines almost without realising what has happened. The castle is taken by a means not at all expected and the three dots are a means by which we, the readers, are taken in unexpectedly. It is also worth commenting on the last word of the third and fourth line: the word "gate" is repeated, whereas elsewhere in the poem the last words of the third and fourth lines merely rhyme. Again this is a technique by which the author draws attention to his meaning. Only after reading this verse are we aware of the irony running through the earlier part of the poem — but more will be said about irony later.

Another important aspect of sound is *onomatopoeia*, where the sound of a word is closely related to the meaning. In *The Castle* there are several onomatopoeia words — "ease", "groan", and, as has been already suggested, even a word such as "wicked".

Rhyme is, of course, what everyone thinks of when poetry is mentioned. To work out a poem's rhyme scheme use the alphabet and repeat a letter at each rhyme, thus:

All through that summer at ease we lay,	*a*
And daily from the turret wall	*b*
We watched the mowers in the hay	*a*
And the enemy half a mile away.	*a*
They seemed no threat to us at all	*b*

This *a b a a b* pattern creates a very compact verse with the last line standing out yet echoing the second line. The rhyme gives the poem an eerie yet romantic feel. Look again at the last verse: it suggests almost a ballad.

How can this shameful tale be told?	*a*
I will maintain until my death	*b*
We could do nothing, being sold;	*a*
Our only enemy was gold,	*a*
And we had no arms to fight it with.	*b*

But, you claim, this time the second and last lines don't rhyme. And you are right — the lines nearly rhyme, and we call that device para-rhyme. It's not that the poet couldn't be bothered to find a rhyming word — he deliberately nearly rhymes the words to create a kind of ghostly, echoing, and almost sad, wistful effect.

But not all poems rhyme — look carefully at the tables on the following pages:

TRADITIONAL AND TWENTIETH CENTURY POETRY

Type of Poem	Description	Characteristics
Traditional	Written in regular verses, called stanzas, with regular rhythm, and regular rhyme	Can use para-rhyme, feminine rhyme, and various kinds of meter, including *iambic pentameter*. Enjambement (run on lines and / or run-on verses)
Sonnet	Poem of 14 lines — sometimes two stanzas where the rhythm of both stanzas is slightly different	Uses the poetic form of 14 lines to heighten the point — often there is a rhyming couplet at the end for dramatic effect
Blank Verse	Written in regular verses, called stanzas, with regular rhythm, but no rhyme	Obviously, does not use rhyming techniques as above, but can use enjambement.
Free Verse	Little regularity — no verses as such, no rhyme, but uses the line to achieve rhythm, but not necessarily a regular rhythm. Still a poem because it is written in lines. Verses sometimes referred to as verse paragraphs	Obviously uses enjambement because it is the line that matters. No rhyming techniques

Type of Poem	Description	Characteristics
Modern Poetry	Difficult to define, but is very similar to and much influenced by Free Verse, but often breaks all kinds of rules, including the rules of punctuation.	e.g, — e e cummings
Concrete Poetry	Where the physical shape of the poem on the page — the typography and layout of the poem — echoes or represents subject matter — i.e, a poem about butterflies would look like a butterfly.	Some of Edwin Morgan's poetry

Blank verse and free verse are important aspects of poetry.

In *The Castle*, Muir breaks all kinds of rules: he ends not only a line, not only a sentence, but the whole poem with a preposition. It has always been considered (wrongly, of course) that to end a sentence with a preposition indicates either a poor education or bad taste on the part of a writer. Churchill, somewhat tongue-in-cheek, claimed "That is something up with which I shall not put" to avoid such a stylistic faux-pas! Muir deliberately ends with "with", so altering the rhythm of the line that he breaks the eerie romantic feel and creates a very 20th century feel instead. The very limpness of the line contrasts with the vibrant, mediaeval imagery of the rest of the poem, and that limpness, that afterthought, makes us realise that the poem isn't just about romantic castles of yesteryear but is also about greed and how all of us, including society as a whole, can be bought — for the right price.

One final point about rhythm and sound when it comes to poetry: the use of the line. One of the big differences between poetry and prose (this book is written in prose) is that poetry is written in deliberate lines, where the line ending is significant. Although prose is also written in lines, the lines are arbitrary — the fact that one line spills on to the next is determined by the word processor and not by the author. Often, in poetry, the line stands by itself — the break at the end of the line sounds quite natural because it's part of the structure not only of the poem but of the sentence. Look again at *The Castle*: almost all the lines stand by themselves. Verse one is like this, as is verse two: the grammatical structure fits the line structure. But note verse three, lines two and three:

> So smooth and high, no man could win
> A foothold there, no clever trick
> Could take us, have us dead or quick.

Here you can see that the grammatical structure does not quite fit the line structure: "A foothold there" spills over on to the next line, as does "could take us". Again, this is a deliberate device called *enjambement* or *run-on lines* which usually creates tension in a poem, because the grammatical structure is being forced into the verse / line structure without quite fitting it. Surprise is created and thus attention is drawn to the meaning. Some poets use this device to quite startling effect.

We have examined a great deal in this chapter and you may well have to read it and reread it several times. The important thing to remember is that when you are studying literature the last thing you want to do is to learn up notes — you should approach the texts you are studying through the three questions set out on page 6:

(a)   What is the text about?
(b)   What effects does it have on me?
(c)   How are the effects achieved?

and this chapter has been very much concerned with all three questions. And that applies to whichever piece of literature you are studying — for your Unit or for the examination itself, including Textual Analysis.

Let's look at another poem, this time by D.H. Lawrence.

BAT

At evening, sitting on this terrace,
When the sun from the west, beyond Pisa, beyond the mountains of Carrara
Departs, and the world is taken by surprise . . .

When the tired flower of Florence is in gloom beneath the glowing
Brown hills surrounding . . .

When under the arches of the Ponte Vecchio
A green light enters against stream, flush from the west,
Against the current of obscure Arno . . .

Look up, and you see things flying
Between the day and the night;
Swallows with spools of dark thread sewing the shadows together.

A circle swoop, and a quick parabola under the bridge arches
Where light pushes through;
A sudden turning upon itself of a thing in the air.
A dip to the water.

And you think:
"The swallows are flying so late!"

Swallows?

Dark air-life looping
Yet missing the pure loop . . .
A twitch, a twitter, an elastic shudder in flight,
And serrated wings against the sky,
Like a glove, a black glove thrown up at the light,
and falling back.

Never swallows!
Bats!
The swallows are gone.

At a wavering instant the swallows gave way to bats
By the Ponte Vecchio . . .
Changing guard.

Bats, and an uneasy creeping in one's scalp
As the bats swoop overhead!
Flying madly.

Pipistrello!
Black piper on an infinitesimal pipe.
Little lumps that fly in air and have voices indefinite, wildly vindictive;

Wings like bits of umbrella.

Bats!

Creatures that hang themselves up like an old rag, to sleep;
And disgustingly upside down.
Hanging upside down like rows of disgusting old rags
And grinning in their sleep.
Bats!

In China the bat is a symbol of happiness

Not for me.

Bat by D.H. Lawrence

You'll agree that this time it is easy to say what this poem is about. It is fairly self-explanatory: the poet is sitting in the evening by the Ponte Vecchio in Florence, Italy. He notices, almost absently, the swallows and then realises, with disgust, that the creatures are not swallows but bats. What is interesting is the way the poet creates the effects he does.

The poem is written in blank verse — there is no rhyme scheme — and it is in free verse — there is no regular rhythm (see Table). The verses are more like paragraphs, and are, in fact, referred to as verse paragraphs. Note how, in the first three verse paragraphs, he creates the feeling of relaxation — the evening, sitting on a terrace, sunset — and the feeling of lethargy — "tired flower of Florence". Each verse is a kind of snapshot or, more accurately, a kind of unfinished painting, the aposiopesis (the three dots) indicating that the reader's imagination has to supply what is missing. Florence was the centre of renaissance art, but is no longer, hence the "tired flower of Florence" — it has passed its best.

He notes the swallows, but it is almost absent-mindedly — "things flying / Between the day and the night". It is not an unpleasant image — "spools of dark thread" which sew the shadows together, a "circle swoop", the "sudden turning upon itself of a thing in the air".

The poet pays a little more attention and muses that the swallows are flying late. Doubt is conveyed by the single line, the single sentence and the question mark: "Swallows?". He begins to notice the detail and the words become unpleasant: "missing the pure loop" — echoing, negatively, "'spool" and "loop". Then really unpleasant words such as "twitch", "twitter", "elastic shudder", "serrated", "a black glove thrown up at the night". The full realisation of truth comes with the single monosyllabic "Bats!" with the hard "b", almost like a swear word and the exclamation mark. The truth brings with it the "uneasy creeping" in his scalp, and his images create feelings of disgust and repulsion: "Little lumps that fly in air", "voices indefinite, wildly vindictive", "Wings like bits of umbrella". That last image is particularly appropriate because of its visual accuracy, especially when he says the wings are like "bits" of umbrella. He uses repetition effectively — in the next line "Bats" repeats (nearly) "bits". I like the cleverness of the next four lines:

> Creatures that hang themselves up like an old rag, to sleep;
> And disgustingly upside down.
> Hanging upside down like rows of disgusting old rags
> And grinning in their sleep.

The repetition of "upside down" in the next line almost creates the impression of *being* upside down, but what is really clever is how he changes the repeated word enough to avoid boredom — "hang" becomes "hanging", and "disgustingly" changes to "disgusting".

Lawrence chooses words very carefully for their connotative area. Why, for example, does he choose "grinning" rather than, say, "smiling"? "Smiling" has a pleasant connotation, whereas "grinning" suggests an underlining mockery, almost threat.

Bat is a simple poem which is technically clever and poetically effective: it captures a bit of experience — a detestation of bats — and recreates the feelings we have for them. It is a very accurate poem.

You can see that we never lose sight of the three questions:

(a)   *What is the poem about?*

(b)   *What effects does it have on me?*

(c)   *How are the effects achieved?*

In many ways, of course, by far the most difficult of these questions is the last one:

How are the effects achieved?

That is the question that is at the basis of Textual Analysis. Of course, you need to be sensitive enough to know what the effect is on you, but, for the purposes of preparing for this Higher, and, really, in order to become a critical and intelligent reader, you need to know how the author has created whatever effect you felt.

Let's try it again, this time with *Lady Lazarus* by Sylvia Plath. Immediate question: who was Lazarus? And therefore who might Lady Lazarus be? Keep the three questions in mind, but we really do want to concentrate on that last question.

LADY LAZARUS

I have done it again.
One year in every ten
I manage it —

A sort of walking miracle, my skin
Bright as a Nazi lampshade,
My right foot

A paperweight,
My face a featureless, fine
Jew linen.

Peel off the napkin
O my enemy.
Do I terrify? —

The nose, the eye pits, the full set of teeth?
The sour breath
Will vanish in a day.

Soon, soon the flesh
The grave cave ate will be
At home on me

And I a smiling woman.
I am only thirty.
And like the cat I have nine times to die.

This is Number Three.
What a trash
To annihilate each decade.

What a million filaments.
The peanut-crunching crowd
Shoves in to see

Them unwrap me hand and foot —
The big strip tease.
Gentlemen, ladies

These are my hands
My knees.
I may be skin and bone,

Nevertheless, I am the same, identical woman.
The first time it happened I was ten.
It was an accident.

The second time I meant
to last it out and not come back at all.
I rocked shut

As a seashell.
They had to call and call
And pick the worms off me like sticky pearls.

Dying
Is an art, like everything else.
I do it exceptionally well.

I do it so it feels like hell.
I do it so it feels real.
I guess you could say I've a call.

It's easy enough to do it in a cell.
It's easy enough to do it and stay put.
It's the theatrical

Comeback in broad day
To the same place, the same face, the same brute
Amused shout:

'A miracle!'
That knocks me out.
There is a charge

For the eyeing of my scars, there is a charge
For the hearing of my heart —
It really goes.

And there is a charge, a very large charge
For a word or a touch
Or a bit of blood

Or a piece of my hair or my clothes.
So, so, Herr Doktor.
So, Herr Enemy.

I am your opus,
I am your valuable,
The pure gold baby

That melts to a shriek.
I turn and burn.
Do not think I underestimate your great concern.

Ash, ash —
You poke and stir.
Flesh, bone, there is nothing there —

A cake of soap,
A wedding ring,
A gold filling.

Herr God, Herr Lucifer
Beware
Beware.

Out of the ash
I rise with my red hair
And I eat men like air.

Lady Lazarus by Sylvia Plath

Have you found out the allusion (reference) to "Lazarus"? You need to know about the story of Lazarus and how Christ raised him from the dead to be able to get the allusion. The title will then be a help to the understanding of the poem.

You need, as always, to establish first of all what the poem is about. Plath is talking about her attempts at committing suicide, and the poem concerns itself with the efforts of the medical profession to pull her round after "Number Three".

Let me give you some help. There are allusions — references — in this poem to the Nazis and to the entertainment industry, references which appear elsewhere in Plath's poetry. She talks of her skin being as "Bright as a Nazi lampshade", her foot being used "as a paperweight": both references to the atrocities Nazis performed on the Jews, where the skin of a Jew was used as a lampshade, and their feet were used as paperweights. She talks about "the big strip tease" (a reference to the removal of her bandages) which "The peanut crunching crowd / shoves in to see" (a reference to the public's casual, uncaring interest in her revival). But with what do we associate "strip tease" and "the peanut crunching crowd"? Yes, you are right, the entertainment industry. What, then, is she saying about what happens to Lady Lazarus when she is revived? How does she feel if the removal of her bandages is like a "strip tease", and if the doctors and hospital staff are like "a peanut crunching crowd" who "shove in to see"? Americans chew peanuts at the cinema or at their version of shows or amusement parks: what does the fact that they are chewing peanuts and shoving their way in to look at her imply about their attitude to her?

But what is really interesting about this poem is in Plath's use of language and poetic technique. Given all that I've said about structure, connotation, rhythm, rhyme, sound, repetition, go through the poem and comment fully on these devices.

Why, towards the end of the poem, does she refer to her doctor as "Herr Doktor" and "Herr Enemy"? What is the image at the end of the poem? Is it appropriate? How does this poem relate to others by Sylvia Plath?

We are asking questions about effects and how they have been created, and as you jot down your answers to these questions in your notebook you are recording your own notes. And much better they will be than any you can buy because your notes record what **you** think and not what someone else thinks. Your genuine reaction to and interest in the literature that you are studying is **exactly** what the examiners are looking for at Higher Level.

But now we must turn to the remaining genre of literature — drama.

CHAPTER SEVEN

DRAMA

Drama forms a vital and important part of any course on literature. Perhaps we should go back to basics and examine the nature of drama. There are various terms we use: "theatre", "the theatre", "drama", "the drama", "stage" "play", "tragedy", "comedy". Each of these words means something quite distinct. A stage is really a lit area. Imagine, for example, you are walking home from school one dark winter's evening along a street of semi-detached houses. You pass by one house — the living room is lit and the curtains are open. You can see in quite easily. Do you stop, just for a look? Of course you do. The lit area is like a stage and the window like a cinema or television screen.

As you watch you notice a young lady coming into the room, wearing a chic, black. backless dress. She walks up to the mantelpiece, lifts a glass of champagne and stands there with her back to the room. Still interested? The door opens again and in walks a young man; he goes up to her, but obviously she is unaware of his presence. He pulls a long knife from his dinner jacket and takes one more step . . .

By this point you are riveted. You have before you all the ingredients of a drama, set on a lit stage: sex, violence, but above all conflict. The windows even have curtains drawn back! What gets your attention is the lit area; the movement helps to keep your attention. These two ingredients alone can halt the most fascinating of conversations: there is nothing quite like a television set switched on high up in a corner of a pub to hold the attention of an open-mouthed crowd stunned into silence by a soap opera with the sound turned off.

No matter how absorbed you are in this book, your attention could easily be distracted by the tip-toeing of a little mouse as it crosses the floor in front of your chair. Movement is a vital ingredient of drama and theatre.

But to keep your attention there has to be conflict. All the plays you know, the films you have seen, the soap operas you couldn't miss, are all based on conflict. Just count the conflict in any of your favourite soap operas at the moment. The conflict is often external — Goodies -v- Baddies, Cowboys -v- Indians. Cops -v- Villains. Often those in conflict are dressed in easily identified uniforms to make the conflict recognisable. The characters involved are simple, almost two-dimensional. cardboard cut-outs. The values involved are stark: the good are very good and the bad are wicked. Not only that but the good get rewarded and the bad get their just deserts.

More complex dramas begin to involve complications — the good aren't always that good and even the baddie can have admirable qualities. Sometimes the dramatist introduces conflict within the hero himself — what we call internal conflict. Much of the drama you are studying for Higher English will involve internal conflict as well as, of course, external conflict. Hamlet is not only in conflict with Claudius, but is in conflict with himself: part of him wants to revenge his father's murder, but another part of him recognises the futility of revenge. Macbeth isn't only in conflict with Malcolm and Macduff; he also recognises, eventually, the futility of his existence and the pointlessness of what he is doing. Willy Loman is in conflict with Biff on the one hand and with the American Dream on the other; but he is also torn internally by his love of the great outdoors and physical labour, and by his ambition to achieve success and fame in the city.

Conflict, then, is the basis of all drama, and conflict can be both external and internal. Your study of plays should begin with an examination of conflict. We call the characters working for the forces of good the "protagonists" and the forces in conflict with the protagonists we call the "antagonistic" forces. Begin by making a list of the protagonists and the antagonistic forces in any play which you are studying. In complex drama the task isn't easy because some characters may well fit into both lists but try it for the texts you are studying. You also have to bear in mind that antagonistic forces are not always characters: Hamlet is in conflict with the social and moral values of the time; John Proctor, in *The Crucible*, is in conflict with the values of the society of which he is a part.

Once you have worked out who is in conflict with whom or with what, you should work out the nature of the conflict: what is the cause of it, how is it expressed, in what ways does it come to a climax, how is the conflict resolved?

There can be many factors which contribute to the conflict, and it can be a complicated job working out the various strands involved. For example, the final major conflict in *Hamlet* is between the mighty opposites Hamlet and Claudius, though, of course, that conflict runs through the whole play. But examine the strands that contribute to that conflict and intensify it.

Conflict is, as has been stressed, the basis of drama, but all drama also involves issues or themes. Remember I said that after you've read a text you should ask yourself what it is about? The answer to that question — and there can be a few answers to the question — gives you the theme — or themes — of the play. Once you have read the text and analysed the conflict as suggested above, you should spend some time thinking out the themes — thinking out what it is that the play says to you. Write down the themes or issues you have decided on, then go back to the text to see which scenes or characters or situations establish the theme or illustrate it or develop it.

One of the major themes in *Macbeth* is duplicity — where appearances are deceptive, where characters are deceitful, where the underlying reality is dangerous, often fatal, and where everything belies the apparently innocent surface:

"Look like the innocent flower, but be the serpent under it."
"False face must hide what the false heart doth know."

"This castle hath a pleasant seat", says Duncan, little realising it is to be the seat of his assassination.

But how does this theme get established in the play? Look carefully at Act I Scene i and examine what the witches say: "Fair is foul and foul is fair" and then look at the first words spoken by Macbeth. As you go through the play you will find many instances where the theme of duplicity is reinforced, and as you find them you should note them down.

But, of course, there are many themes in the plays that you are likely to be studying for Higher English. Most of these themes are well known, but you may detect in your favourite play themes that other people haven't written about: all that matters is that you can justify whatever theme you want to write about with evidence from the text to support your argument. The same applies to your opinion of the characters. You may well believe that Hamlet is a moody, spoiled, self-centred little brat who, because his comfortable little world is upset by his mother's remarriage, tries to make life difficult for his stepfather, hoping his interference will end it all. This isn't a conventional view, but it is one which could be sustained by a careful reading of the play.

Equally, Hamlet can be thought of as an intelligent intellectual whose integrity and moral values are out of step with and even ahead of the times in which he lives. While the others, such as Laertes and Fortinbras, accept the simplistic revenge-philosophy of the time, Hamlet questions the very concept of revenge itself. Again this view can be supported by the text. You make up your mind what you think as long as you can back up what you think from your knowledge of and by relevant references to the play.

Your study of a play, then, must include a study of conflict, a working-out of themes, an informed knowledge of the characters, and an understanding of the role of the setting. All this takes time and effort, and has to be done at the time you are reading the texts in class.

In addition to all this, you should work your way through the following assignment sheet, the answers to which will provide you with your own notes for revision before the exam.

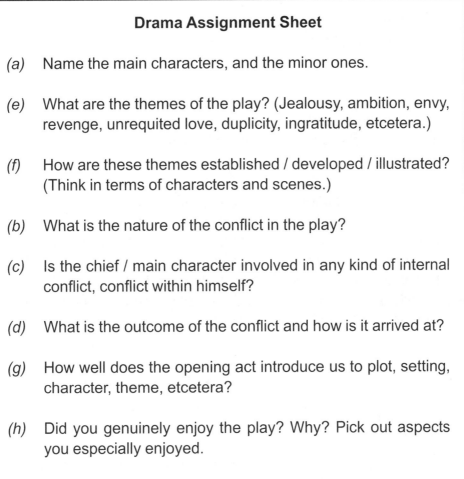

Drama Assignment Sheet

(a)   Name the main characters, and the minor ones.

(e)   What are the themes of the play? (Jealousy, ambition, envy, revenge, unrequited love, duplicity, ingratitude, etcetera.)

(f)   How are these themes established / developed / illustrated? (Think in terms of characters and scenes.)

(b)   What is the nature of the conflict in the play?

(c)   Is the chief / main character involved in any kind of internal conflict, conflict within himself?

(d)   What is the outcome of the conflict and how is it arrived at?

(g)   How well does the opening act introduce us to plot, setting, character, theme, etcetera?

(h)   Did you genuinely enjoy the play? Why? Pick out aspects you especially enjoyed.

(i)   What do you feel you learned from studying the play?

But we also have to think about dramatic technique. A dramatic text is obviously intended for performance, but you are studying the *text* and not the performance. Therefore every aspect of that text matters — including the stage instructions, which are often intended for actors and producers to help them achieve what the dramatist wants in performance, but sometimes these stage instructions are also intended for the general reader. Look carefully at the stage instructions in *The Crucible* or *Death of a Salesman* and you will see what I mean. In the latter play, Miller talks about the music — a flute — *insinuating* itself. The use of such a verb is intended to convey mood and not just a simple instruction.

Another aspect that you need to study is how character is revealed in drama. Often it is done by means of what is said and through action — not necessarily by the words and actions of the character in question, but by the words and actions of other characters.

Theme, too, is often revealed not just by the interaction of character with setting, but through the words and actions of the characters.

A vital aspect of dramatic technique is dramatic irony, a device which is highly effective in revealing character, theme, and situation. But it is often effective in building up the drama — helping to create climax, an important aspect of drama. Dramatic irony occurs where at least one character on stage is not fully aware of what is happening or the implications of what is happening, whereas the audience is fully aware of such implications. Take *Macbeth* for example: we have already noted the part where Duncan says,

> This castle has a pleasant seat,
> The air doth nimbly and sweetly recommend itself
> Unto our gently senses.

The audience knows that Duncan is about to be murdered within the castle whereas Duncan is blissfully unaware of his fate.

Another perfect example of dramatic irony is when John Proctor, challenged to recite the Ten Commandments, manages to remember nine of them but falls to remember the Commandment forbidding adultery, the one sin that he has committed and which will bring about his ultimate downfall.

Dramatic irony is often used to illuminate or dramatise the theme of a play and, as such, is an important dramatic technique.

This is a chapter which has asked you to do many things. If you do all that it has asked, then you will be well prepared.

We have examined drama in much detail, we've gone back to basics and asked ourselves what drama is all about. Success here, as in everything in life, has to do with the amount of preparation you put in: we **must** spend time on preparing **how** to **study** drama, prose, poetry before we go on to look at how you answer the questions set in the examination.

CHAPTER EIGHT

SPECIALIST STUDY

(Literature)

Although the Specialist Study is no longer externally assessed, nevertheless it remains a vital part of your Higher English course. The process of conducting a piece of personal investigation, between 1200 and 1800 words long, into a work of literature or Media Studies will not only prepare you well for the two critical essay questions in the examination itself but will teach you a great deal about how to analyse and evaluate literary texts.

Your Study should take the form of a detailed investigation of a single literary text or set of short texts or a comparison of two or more texts. You should choose your own text; your choice should be made from imaginative literature, biography, memoirs, essays or journalism. You may compare a literary text with its non-print version: for example, you may compare a novel with its film adaptation.

The task sounds utterly daunting, but if you follow my advice then you should find it more straightforward than you at first imagine. And remember, you only have to pass this aspect of the course — you do not have to strive for an A grade, though of course you should strive to achieve your best.

One thing you must do is plan how you set about tackling your SSL: what you must not and cannot do is to leave everything to the last minute. And by last minute, I mean the beginning of March. You really have to begin the work for your SSL as early as you possibly can.

You ask: *Where do I begin?* and *How should I begin?* Well, you really must begin by thinking about the kinds of books, plays, and poems that you have so far enjoyed studying in English. One of the main keys to success in the SSL is to be interested and involved in the text that is going to be the basis of your study. Your interest really does have to be genuine. And the text really does have to be your own choice.

CHOOSING THE TEXT

You must choose for yourself the text on which you want to work. You may consult your teacher about that choice, but the important thing to remember is that your teacher is not allowed to choose the text for you. The study has to be based on your personal reading.

Begin the job of choosing as early as you can: certainly have your choice made by the September of the year before you are to sit the examination. You should start by thinking of the kinds of texts that you enjoyed reading and studying in your Fourth Year. I shall guess, and there's a pretty good chance that I am right, that you will choose prose: a novel or some short stories. My advice to you is to think again. Since the vast majority of SSLs involve the novel, you would do well to think about poetry or drama. There are far too few SSLs which have poetry or drama as their basis, and you should give some consideration to any poems you have recently grown to like or to a play that has caught your imagination. But please do not think about using texts that you have studied the year before. You must choose material that is fresh to you.

Another thing: you should avoid basing your SSL on works of very popular fiction; not because I think that such texts are inferior, but because it is difficult to find much to say about them — and remember you have to find 1200–1800 words. If the text you have chosen is an easy read, then the chances are that it is not a very demanding text, and as such you will find that there is not a lot you can write about it. My advice, then, is that the more challenging the text, the more you will be able to write. And, ironically, the more interested you are likely to become in it.

Another word of warning. A very popular choice for SSLs by many candidates is non-fiction — biography / autobiography / travel books, and while such a choice is not a problem in itself, what can be a major problem is the confusion that can occur in the process of writing the SSL. When writing about non-fiction, you have to remember that you are not discussing the experiences of the author — what kind of person he/she is or the nature of the country in the case of a travel book.

You still have to deal with the techniques used by the author: you are analysing the effects achieved by the author and you must not confuse an English study with psychology or sociology! Be very careful if you decide to make non-fiction the subject of your SSL — too many easily fail.

OK, you ask, what things should I bear in mind when I am choosing the text for my SSL? Let me list some advice:

(a)   The book, play, or poem (and please remember what I have said about choosing poetry and drama) must interest you — do not choose to write about a text that bores you because you will communicate that boredom in your writing.

Higher (and Intermediate) Level English demand evidence of personal interest in and engagement with the texts you have chosen to write about, not just here, but in the Critical Essay as well. You must demonstrate in your SSL that you like the text you have chosen and that it has said something of interest to you. If you don't, it is conceivable that you may not pass.

(b)   The text you choose must be able to provide you with plenty to write about.

You may enjoy a popular text that is easy to read, but it may not stimulate you into writing much. A more "difficult" text will offer you plenty on which you can comment.

(c)   The text must have something to say to you as a person.

The text you choose must have something to say to you personally. Maybe there is a character with whom you identify, a setting with which you are familiar, a situation you recognise, or a theme that means a lot to you. You must personally choose the text, and you must personally be involved in it.

Let us now assume that you have chosen the text and that it meets all three of the requirements above. What next? Well, you must become very familiar with the text: read it over and over again until your knowledge of it is thorough. Oh, and you must buy yourself a little notebook! Then you set yourself the famous three questions:

(a) What is the text about?

(b) What effects does it have on me?

(c) How has the author achieved these effects?

The answer to (a) above is very important when it comes to the SSL, because the answer to this question will provide you with the themes that the novel, play, or poem has for you. Remember, don't answer this question in terms of plot: remember my advice about answering this question — theme not plot. One advantage of studying poetry for your SSL is that you will be less inclined to want to retell plot since, by and large, poems don't really have plots. Candidates who tackle novels (the majority — remember) often find it difficult to tear themselves away from the plot!

Answer our question, then, in terms of *themes*. For example, you might jot down in your notebook that your chosen poem is about *the turmoil of youth* or about how we *become victims of old age* or about *unrequited love* or about *jealousy*. You now have your theme, and the point is that it really is *your* theme: you are declaring your personal interest in the text by saying what it is about for you.

Once you have stated the theme or themes, you have to go on and say how these themes are established and developed. Let's say that you have chosen a poem. Look at the very beginning. Where does the poet establish the theme you have chosen to write about? How does he go on to develop that theme? Does he add to it, qualify it, exemplify it? Note down all your answers.

Now, of course, you are not expected to be the world's most sensitive and most perspicacious reader. Even someone as experienced and as clever as your teacher had to consult other people at sometime in his / her career when studying texts. You may have noticed yourself that, after having seen a film or a television play with a friend, as you begin to talk to each other about it, your ideas about it may change or become more definite or more developed. It is not forbidden to talk to your teacher about your poem, to chat over with him / her the ideas you have so far thought about. Nor is it forbidden to consult the better quality commercially-produced notes. What is unwise is to depend on your teacher or those notes for your ideas, and what is absolutely forbidden is for you to copy down what your teacher has said or to copy out the notes you have bought. The ideas have to be your own, but there is no harm in talking them over with an expert or consulting what an expert has written. This whole process should be about building up your relationship with your chosen text and not depending on someone else's. Your answer to question *(b)* will help you — note your reactions to the text as you go along.

Next, we have to think about author technique: in other words we have to answer the third question — how does the author achieve the effects?

Perhaps the most interesting area when it comes to the study of literature is the area of author technique. Let's start with yourself. Since you were at primary school, you have been asked to write essays and to create short stories; in other words, for about ten or twelve years now you have been striving to be an accomplished author. So, how do you go about your writing? Let us be even more specific: you have been set a task by your teacher to write about the theme of jealousy and how it can affect friendship, and you have been told that you can choose to write either discursively or creatively. How do you begin? Clearly, you have to begin by making choices. And the first choice has to be: *Am I going to write a discursive essay on the nature of jealousy within friendship or is it going to be a short story with such a topic as its theme?* Let us assume that you have chosen to write a short story. What next? Again you are faced with choices — choices to do with where you are going to set the story, when you are going to set it, who are the main characters, and, possibly most importantly, what is going to happen.

The point I am really trying to make is that stories, novels, plays, poems, whatever, don't just *occur*: someone, quite deliberately, puts them together in a certain order and in a certain way. You do that when you write, as do all authors. We as readers, as critical readers, can study just how these stories, novels, plays and poems have been put together. In so doing, we are studying *author technique* and that is precisely what you have to do next for your SSL — study author technique. By now you will have realised that we are answering the third question:

(c) How has the author achieved these effects?

This question is to do with Textual Analysis: the examination of the ways in which the author has created the effects that he has had on you. If you have chosen to study a poem for your SSL, then by now you have made your notes on the themes suggested by the poem, the effects created by the poet, and the ways in which he created those effects. And you have got these notes by answering the three questions as set out previously.

But I am now going to give you a strong word of warning about Textual Analysis techniques when writing your SSL. Textual Analysis *ought* to be about the analysis of the ways in which the author has created his or her various effects, which, in turn, are related to theme. If, however, in preparing for textual analysis you concentrate almost exclusively on the techniques (ignoring theme), then there is the danger that all you write about are the techniques and you will forget about the theme. I have seen this done too many times – do not become so bogged down in detail that you forget what the text is actually about. The worst example I have come across is one student who, writing about a novel, commented on the author's skilful use of enjambement! Needless to say, the candidate failed.

The way to avoid such a pitfall is to have an appropriate task for your SSL. If you set yourself a task which allows you to deal with theme, then you won't be tempted into silly, irrelevant, unrelated comments about techniques.

SETTING THE TASK

In all my years of experience as an examiner and marker of Higher English, I am still astonished at the number of candidates who fail to set themselves tasks. I cannot stress enough how important it is to have a task and to stick to it. Too many candidates just set off writing the SSL which ends up as a kind of vague book review with hardly a chance of passing.

Your teacher is not allowed to set the task for you, but of course he / she is allowed to give you advice about the task you want to tackle. It may be that in his / her opinion the task you have chosen is too easy or too difficult or else your teacher may feel that it won't allow you to demonstrate all the skills that you have acquired. The task, however, must interest you; it must be such that it will get you engaged in the writing process and allow you to demonstrate that engagement as you write. Above all, it should be specific. Here are some examples of successful tasks:

♦   A comparative evaluation of the poetic techniques by which Wilfred Owen in *Anthem for Doomed Youth* and *Exposure* and Isaac Rosenberg in *Break of Day in the Trenches* portray images of war.

♦   The ways in which Emily Brontë uses narrative structure, setting, and characterisation in her novel *Wuthering Heights* to explore the nature of cruelty.

♦   A critical evaluation of the techniques (including setting and characterisation) by which William Golding portrays the theme of leadership in his novel *Lord of the Flies*.

♦   The ways in which Kurt Vonnegut uses structure, characterisation, and humour in his novel *Slapstick* to attack North American values.

♦   The ways in which Joseph Heller uses paradox to explore his theme of the insanity of war and USAF management in *Catch-22*.

You will see that all of these titles are highly specific, which should help you to stay relevant.

If you have done your note-taking thoroughly and conscientiously, then the task should suggest itself. You should have an idea of what it is you want to say about the text you have studied.

Let us now suppose that you have done all the preparation, you have selected your task, and you are well into the writing of your SSL. The next thing that you will want to know is if you are on the right lines. What is it, you may well be asking, that is expected of you? Fortunately, the question is easy to answer. To begin with, you should put that question to your teacher because your school will have in its possession a document from the Scottish Qualifications Authority explaining in great detail how the SSL is to be assessed. I can put it very simply for you: what is being looked for is exactly the same as what is looked for in a Critical Essay:

(a) *Your knowledge of the text.* You must show in your SSL that you have read the text and are familiar with it.

(b) *Your understanding of the ideas in the text.* You must show that you understand the ideas — themes — dealt with by the text. And, of course, remember that these are the themes personal to you — what you understand the text to be about.

(c) *Your understanding of the author's techniques.* You must make it clear that you are familiar with the various techniques deployed by the author — what we talked about above. Don't just quote a bit and then say "isn't that a lovely metaphor" or "what an exciting bit of onomatopoeia". Say instead what is appropriate about the metaphor or what effect has been achieved by the onomatopoeia — and how these techniques relate to the portrayal of theme.

(d) *Your genuine personal interest.* This is what I have been stressing all along. You must demonstrate that you have been involved in the text and have got something out of it. Without evidence of genuine personal interest, is unlikely that the SSL will pass. Your personal interest must run through your entire SSL and cannot be achieved by tagging on a paragraph at the end that states — "By the way I really liked this book because it reminded me of my old grandmother and the things she told me she did when she was a young girl in Dublin". That is NOT what is meant by personal interest! If you have chosen a text that genuinely interests you and have set yourself a task that will focus your line of thought, your enthusiasm for it will come through your writing. Personal interest should be implicit throughout your SSL and not explicitly stated.

Finally, you should remember that the stipulated word length is between 1200 and 1800 words. Don't sell yourself short by producing a mere 800 words, but on the other hand please limit your SSL to a maximum of 1800 words. If your SSL is too long, look, again at the first page because if there is anywhere that you can wield a blue pencil, I am willing to wager that it's there. Too often in the first page, candidates waste words recounting plot: if you have done that, get rid of it. It is comment that matters not a rehash of the text.

Do bear in mind all that has been said in this chapter, and please do not read it in isolation from the rest of this book. You need to know a great deal about how to study literature and that topic is a matter for more than this chapter alone.

CHAPTER NINE

THE OTHER ASSESSMENTS

Higher English assessment is in two parts: the examination — Paper I, which consists of Interpretation or Close Reading and Paper II, which consists of two Critical Essays. But there are compulsory internal assessments for literature, the SSL and Textual Analysis.

TEXTUAL ANALYSIS

In many ways this book has been all about Textual Analysis. It is the most important skill to develop if you want to become a critical and intelligent reader of books, poetry, journals and newspapers. I also very firmly believe that the only way to teach literature and the only way to study it is through the continual development of Textual Analysis skills. Otherwise you merely reiterate what someone else thinks about the text in question, and that can be satisfactory for no-one. I have also included the warning about Textual Analysis — it is not about identifying literary devices in isolation! Everything must be related to the theme of the work you are analysing.

You must make up your own mind about the texts you have chosen to study. But you aren't out there entirely on your own — there is a framework which will help you form your ideas: the three questions.

(a)	What is the text about? *[Answer in themes.]*
(b)	What effects does it have on me? *[Answer in terms of your reactions — laugh, cry, felt sad, etcetera.]*
(c)	How has the author created these effects? *[Answer in terms of techniques.]*

If you bear these questions — and the answers to them — in mind, you will be well-prepared for the Textual Analysis assessment and for the Critical Essays in the examination itself.

THE CRITICAL ESSAY

What far too many candidates do in their preparation for this paper is to buy a set of commercially produced notes, digest them in their entirety, and regurgitate them on the day of the examination, no matter what the question asks. If you have studied your chosen texts in the way in which I have recommended then you have no need to purchase anyone else's ideas because you will have plenty of your own.

As with your preparation for the SSL, make your own notes from the very beginning. Decide for yourself what the themes of your chosen texts are, what issues they deal with. Then decide how these themes get established, how they are developed, what role the characters play, what significance the setting has, etcetera. In other words, as you answer *(a)*, *(b)* and *(c)* on page 91, write down your responses — they will form the basis of your own notes, which will have the merit of being your own and therefore highly personal — a demand of this examination.

There are three main reasons for most of the failures in this part of the examination, and they are all related to the over-use of commercially produced notes:

    (i)   not answering the question asked;

    (ii)   not giving a personal response;

    (iii)   not producing a sufficiently adequate answer.

If you have spent money, time and effort mugging up what somebody terribly important has had to say about *Macbeth* or *Death of a Salesman*, then the temptation to write all that you have learned down in the examination is almost impossible to overcome. Yet, all those hard-conned notes, pitchforked into your answer because you spent hours learning them, far from helping you in your time of need are, in fact, the cause of your downfall. Examiners are experts at detecting notes — the ideas themselves and the way that they are expressed are so obviously not the candidate's own. Notes, almost by definition, prevent you from expressing your opinion about the book, and, as I have told you repeatedly, there are many marks available for expressing a personal response. And if you are dependent on notes, you will run out of ideas in your answer, producing a short, inadequate response that is derivative and devoid of personal involvement.

What should I do then? Look carefully at the question. In many ways, the examination is now more helpful than it has ever been previously. The questions are presented in terms of theme and then you are directed to examine the techniques by which the theme is portrayed. You should then select from your own knowledge of the text what is relevant in answering the demands of the question, and ensure that you communicate to the examiner some enthusiasm for the text in your response.

But I have to give you a word of warning. Although the questions are perhaps more helpful than they have ever been in that they are designed to keep you relevant, nevertheless they are more specific than they have ever been. You cannot get away with knowing only two texts — one poem and a short story — on the hope that they will "fit" a question. Because the questions are so specific, there is no longer any guarantee (if ever there was) that *Assisi* or *Lamb to the Slaughter* will get you through Higher English. Look carefully at the recent Critical Essay questions and you will see what I mean. You need to know a range and variety of texts from more than one genre to ensure success.

And look over everything I have said about the SSL. There are only three differences between the SSL and the Critical Essay: the length, the number of marks and the fact that in the SSL you have to devise your own task whereas in the Critical Essay you are given the task.

In your Critical Essay answer, you have to demonstrate that you have a sound knowledge of the text, that you can analyse and evaluate the writer's techniques, that you can remain relevant to the question asked, and that you can write formally and correctly. Always begin your answer with the wording of the question and keep referring to the question throughout your answer — that way, you will remain relevant.

As with everything else, the secret lies in being well prepared, of course, but also in planning your answer before you start to write it. The readiness is all.

CONCLUSION

Literature, if we know how to read it, can tell us something about ourselves, about life, about the nature of existence itself. Reading *Hamlet* isn't quite the same thing as reading the side of an HP Sauce bottle: *Hamlet* is more demanding — it requires a higher level reading skill. The main purpose of this book is to help you develop as many reading skills as you can, though a book can only begin the process. The rest is up to you. You must practise reading the way that you practise any other skill if you want to keep it in shape.

This book has also been about preparing your literature studies for your Higher English course and examination, though I hasten to add that the sole purpose of literature is not so that candidates will beat out their brains in some desperate examination hall or so that some poor marker can find, in an even more desperate study, solace in the fact that he knows the exact words that Macbeth said and has a red pen to prove it.

Literature isn't some geometric theorem to be conned by rote and recited at will. But the examination has to be prepared for, like it or not, and this book aims to make that preparation easier and a little more palatable. The only method is by the close study of your chosen text. Think out for yourself what the themes or issues are for you, and then work out what scenes, characters, images establish, illustrate and develop those themes. Such a close study of the text will, at the same time, develop your skills at Textual Analysis, and as you develop such skills you will learn to read with greater sensitivity, understanding and awareness. Nothing is in compartments in English; each skill affects the development of the other.

In your answers, choose the questions that best suit the texts that you have studied, be relevant, answer exactly what is asked, write formally, be genuine, and, above all, refer very closely to the text itself to demonstrate to the examiner your knowledge and your understanding. Never make a point about a book without backing it up with evidence from the text. And remember, literature is there to challenge our ideas, to help us develop as human beings, to enrich our lives, and, above all, to be enjoyed.

Remember that, and tell the examiner about it in the month of May.

ACKNOWLEDGEMENTS

We hereby acknowledge the use of copyright material in this book
and are grateful to those for granting this permission.

Extract from *Under Milkwood*
by Dylan Thomas and published by J.M. Dent.
Reprinted by permission of David Higham Associates.

Afternoons from *Collected Poems*
by Philip Larkin.
Reprinted by permission of The Society of Authors as the
Literary Representative of the Estate of Philip Larkin.

Extract from *Shooting an Elephant*
by George Orwell (Copyright © George Orwell, 1936.).
Reprinted by permission of Bill Hamilton as the Literary Executor of the
Estate of the Late Sonia Brownell Orwell and Secker & Warburg Ltd.

Extract from *The Power and the Glory*
by Graham Greene and published by Random House.
Reprinted by permission of David Higham Associates.

The Castle from *Collected Poems*
by Edwin Muir.
Reprinted by permission of the publisher Faber & Faber Ltd.

Extract from *Break of Day in the Trenches*
by Isaac Rosenberg

Bat
by D.H. Lawrence (1885–1930)

Lady Lazarus
by Sylvia Plath

I should like to express my sincere gratitude to Alice and Tom Ferrie, whose careful reading of the text provided perspicacious suggestions, while at the same time removing a number of errors and infelicities of expression. I should also like to thank Kevin Bolton, without whose constant support and encouragement this book would never have been written.

Printed by Bell & Bain Ltd., Glasgow, Scotland, U.K.